W9-BUG-570

The Ultimate Weapon

The test of the first bomb at Alamogordo, New Mexico, in July 1945 (National Archives)

The Ultimate Weapon

The Race to Develop the Atomic Bomb

Edward T. Sullivan

Holiday House / New York

To Milton Meltzer for raising the bar so high and inspiring me to reach for it

To the helpful staff of the Oak Ridge Public Library, who assisted me in my research. To Ed Westcott, whose photographs are featured throughout this book. To the many veterans of the Manhattan Project who generously shared their experiences with me. To Regina Griffin, my tough, insightful editor, and her helpful assistant, Meghan Day. To all my friends and colleagues who offered encouragement and support. To Judy for her encouragement, love, patience, support, and willingness to read so many drafts.

Book design by John Grandits
Map on page 30 by Heather Saunders,
based on a map originated by MPHPA

Printed in the United States of America
www.holidayhouse.com
First Edition
1 3 5 7 9 10 8 6 4 2

Library of Congress Cataloging-in-Publication Data
Sullivan, Edward T., 1966–
The ultimate weapon : the race to develop the atomic bomb/
by Edward T. Sullivan.—1st ed.
p. cm.
Includes bibliographical references and index.
ISBN-13: 978-0-8234-1855-8
ISBN-10: 0-8234-1855-3
1. Atomic bomb—United States—History. 2. Manhattan Project
(U.S.)—History. I. Title.
QC773.3.U5S85 2006
355.8'25119'0973—dc22
2005050330

Contents

Well, I'm gonna preach you a sermon 'bout Old Man Atom,
I don't mean the Adam in the Bible datum.
I don't mean the Adam that Mother Eve mated,
I mean the thing that science liberated.
Einstein says he's scared,
And when Einstein's scared, I'm scared.

Hiroshima, Nagasaki, Alamogordo, Bikini . . .

—Irving Bibo

Lieutenant Colonel Paul W. Tibbets, Jr., waves from the cockpit of the Enola Gay *before taking off on August 6, 1945, to drop the atomic bomb on Hiroshima. (National Archives)*

Introduction
Weapons of Mass Destruction

My God, what have we done?
—Captain Robert Lewis, *Enola Gay* copilot

A camera crew surrounded Lieutenant Colonel Paul Tibbets as he stepped from the truck onto the runway. He had been warned there would be "a little publicity," but the cameras and lights made the scene look like a Hollywood production. The crew members of the *Enola Gay* B-29 bomber found themselves being treated as if they were movie stars—a surprising situation given that the airplane was taking part in one of the best kept secrets in military history. The crew knew its mission was unlike any other ever undertaken. At a briefing two days earlier, navy captain William Parsons had explained: "The bomb you are about to drop is something new in the history of warfare. It is the most destructive weapon ever produced. We think it will knock out almost everything within a three-mile area." What the *Enola Gay* crew would do would forever change the nature of warfare.

Enola Gay departed from the small Pacific island of Tinian at 2:45 A.M. local time on Monday, August 6, 1945. Two escort planes would accompany it on its mission. On board the *Enola Gay* was "Little Boy," a

Commander A. F. Birch labels "Little Boy" unit L-11 before loading it on a trailer at the assembly building on the island of Tinian. (National Archives)

uranium-fueled atomic bomb. Hiroshima, a city in Japan, home to approximately 320,000 people, was the target.

The weather was perfect. By 8:13 A.M., the Japanese army issued an alert that three large enemy planes had been spotted. At 8:15 A.M., Major Thomas Ferebee pressed a switch to release "Little Boy." Less than sixty seconds later, there was a blinding flash of light that grew into a purple fireball. Two shock waves hit the plane. A massive cloud thousands of feet high rose into the sky, forming what looked like a giant mushroom. The three planes did not lose sight of the enormous mushroom cloud until they were 363 miles away. Sergeant Bob Caron, *Enola Gay*'s tail gunner, was the only crew member looking directly at the bomb when it exploded. He described what he saw:

The bomb explodes above Hiroshima. (National Archives)

> A column of smoke is rising fast. It has a fiery red core. A bubbling mass, purple gray in color with that red core. It's all turbulent. Fires are springing up everywhere, like flames shooting out of a huge bed of coals. . . . Here it comes, the mushroom shape. . . . It's maybe a mile or two wide and a half mile high. . . . It's very black, but there is a purplish tint to the cloud. . . . The flames and smoke are billowing out, whirling out into the foothills. The hills are disappearing under the smoke.

Colonel Tibbets radioed Tinian: "Mission successful."

On the ground, a schoolboy named Shintaro Fukuhara was watching his little brother try to catch a dragonfly when he was blinded by a flash of light. His body burned as if it had been thrown into a furnace and his skin turned deep red, the color of a cooked lobster.

"Fat Man" is placed on a trailer in front of the assembly building on Tinian. (National Archives)

The destructive power of "Little Boy" was stunning. Everything within two square miles of ground zero was cremated. More than 96 percent of the buildings in Hiroshima were either destroyed or heavily damaged. Tens of thousands of people, the majority of them civilians, were killed instantly. Tens of thousands more died a short time later from radiation poisoning. By the end of December 1945, the death toll reached 140,000. By 1950, the total death toll reached 200,000.

On August 9, 1945, three days following the bombing of Hiroshima, the United States executed an equally devastating attack on the Japanese city of Nagasaki. The B-29 bomber *Bockscar* dropped the plutonium-fueled "Fat Man" atomic bomb, instantly killing 40,000 people and leaving the city in ruins. The death toll reached 70,000 in January 1948. By 1950 the total death toll reached 140,000. It was the second time an atomic bomb, the most destructive weapon ever used, was unleashed against a wartime enemy.

The purpose of dropping the bombs was to bring to a swift end World War II, the bloodiest and most destructive conflict of the twentieth century. The plan worked. On August 15, 1945, Emperor Hirohito announced the unconditional surrender of Japan to his people. World War II was over.

The creation of the atomic bomb was the culmination of an extraordinary three-year race to be the first to possess it. This race involved more than one hundred thousand Americans, both civilian and military, who worked seven days a week around the clock in an environment shrouded in intense secrecy and tight security. It was called the Manhattan Project.

The USS Shaw *explodes during the Japanese raid on Pearl Harbor, December 7, 1941. (National Archives)*

One
The Race for the Bomb

The decisive assaults upon mankind now proceed
from the drawing boards and laboratory.
—Alfred Doblin, German novelist

When the forces of Imperial Japan attacked United States military bases in Hawaii on December 7, 1941, the world was already at war. Germany, under the dictatorship of Adolf Hitler, had conquered much of Europe. Since 1939, Great Britain had stood almost alone against Germany, but in June 1941, Hitler invaded the Soviet Union, which had opened another front in the war. On the other side of the world, Japan had been pursuing expansion in the Far East since the turn of the twentieth century, occupying Korea since 1910; Manchuria, a region of China, in 1931; and conquering most of China's major coastal cities by 1941.

In 1940 Japan had signed the Tripartite, or Axis Pact, which allied it with Nazi Germany and Italy, whose leader was the Fascist dictator Benito Mussolini. Although not Fascist, Japan's militaristic government had strong interests in territorial expansion in East Asia, as Germany and Italy did in Europe. The German conquest of France in 1940 allowed Japan to occupy the formerly French-controlled areas of South-

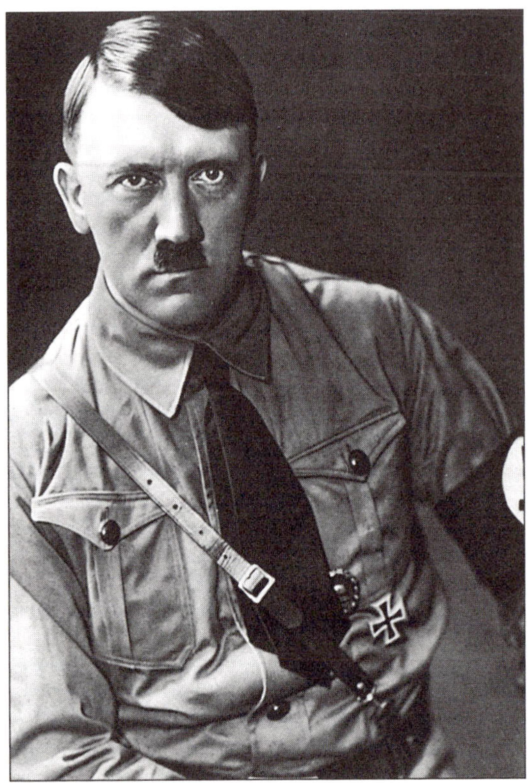

*Adolf Hitler,
dictator of Nazi Germany,
1933–1945
(Library of Congress)*

east Asia, such as Vietnam. The raw materials these territories produced were crucial to sustaining the Japanese war machine. Alarmed by Japanese aggression in the Far East, the United States had imposed embargoes on oil and other resources that were vital to Japan. When diplomatic negotiations failed to lift the embargoes, Japan prepared for war.

On December 7, 1941, forces of the Japanese navy launched a surprise attack against the United States naval base at Pearl Harbor and other military installations in Hawaii. The attack was devastating. The American Pacific fleet was crippled. The Japanese military knew their country could not match the economic or technological power of the United States, but they gambled that the psychological impact of the Pearl Harbor disaster would leave Americans with no stomach to fight.

Japan launched simultaneous invasions all over the Pacific, including the American-controlled Philippine Islands, as well as Malaya, Thai-

REMEMBER PEARL HARBOR
CRUSH THEM!
A HILTS' CARTOON
HILTS PUBLISHING CO., NIAGARA FALLS, N. Y. AND DAYTONA BEACH, FLORIDA

A propaganda poster featuring the heads of Emperor Hirohito of Japan (left), Adolf Hitler, and Italian dictator Benito Mussolini (right) on the body of a snake (Library of Congress)

land, Guam, and Wake Island. France and the Netherlands, already defeated by the Germans in 1940, had proven unable to defend their Asian territories. Great Britain, busy fighting Germany, did not have the resources to defend its own Asian possessions properly. Within a few months, the Japanese occupied a large part of East Asia, including islands in the Dutch East Indies, Hong Kong, Singapore, and Southeast Asia. They were now in a position to threaten Australia, New Zealand, Burma, and India.

Before the attack on Pearl Harbor, the United States had maintained an official policy of neutrality, despite the conflicts raging in both Asia and Europe. Congress had empowered President Franklin Delano Roosevelt to establish the Lend-Lease program, which allowed the United States to supply economic and material aid to the British and Soviets to help them hold out against Germany, but that was the extent

President Roosevelt signs the declaration of war against Japan. (Library of Congress)

of U.S. involvement in the war. In response to the surprise attack on Pearl Harbor, the U.S. government and the vast majority of the public wholeheartedly supported a declaration of war on Japan. Its allies—Germany and Italy—responded by declaring war on the U.S.

The United States now faced the considerable burden of fighting two formidable military powers in two very different parts of the world. Germany and Japan were already battle hardened. They possessed experienced soldiers and field-tested equipment. They had built up massive stockpiles of war materials years before they had gone to war, and their economies and industries were already focused on war production.

The United States would have to race to catch up. The remarkably short time it took to do this was achieved through the willingness of Americans to make extraordinary sacrifices for the war effort.

Germany was developing new, secret weapons, such as a rocket that could carry bombs across the English Channel, and airplanes with jet engines. Especially troubling were reports that German scientists were experimenting with splitting the atom. Scientists believed that splitting an atom—breaking apart the nucleus of an atom—would release an enormous amount of energy. If Germany were successful in developing nuclear weapons, it could conquer the world.

In 1938 two physicists at the Kaiser Wilhelm Institute in Berlin, Germany—Otto Hahn and Fritz Strassmann—discovered that by bombarding atoms of the element uranium with neutrons, they could actually split the atoms, a process called fission. These two scientists based their experiments on the work of Albert Einstein, the German physicist most famous for determining that the energy in matter is equal to matter's mass multiplied by the speed of light squared ($E = mc^2$).

Otto Hahn
(Atomic Archive)

Fritz Strassmann
(Atomic Archive)

Dr. Lise Meitner, an Austrian physicist. In 1944, Otto Hahn received the Nobel Prize in Chemistry for discovering nuclear fission, but Meitner, who collaborated with Hahn on the discovery, was never awarded the Nobel Prize. (Library of Congress)

Scientists had for some time theorized that atomic fission was possible. Hahn and Strassmann conducted experiments with uranium and discovered that the uranium atoms split into different elements, releasing a tremendous amount of energy in the process. Fellow scientists Otto Frisch and Lise Meitner calculated that energy to be 200 million electron volts, an immense amount. Scientists later realized that pound for pound, fission could produce more than 20 million times the energy of the powerful explosive TNT!

When Hahn and Strassmann made their discovery, there were few top physicists still working in Germany. During the 1920s and early 1930s, Germany had been the center of the scientific world, and physicists from around the globe had come to Göttingen University to work and study with renowned physicists such as Max Born, James Franck, and Werner Heisenberg. But Germany had lost many of its prominent scientists, artists, composers, and other professionals and scholars in the years after Adolf Hitler was appointed chancellor by President Paul von Hindenburg in 1933.

Throughout the 1930s, Hitler undermined Germany's democratic government to establish one of the most ruthless regimes in history. His party, the National Socialist German Workers' Party, or Nazi Party, began to control every aspect of German society and culture, including the universities. Professors were given an ultimatum: join the Nazi Party and adopt its racism or lose their positions. Those professors who were Jewish were not given the choice of joining the party—they lost their jobs and their other rights.

The Nazis persecuted all Jews. They gradually stripped Jews of not only their right to work, but also their right to own property and practice their religion. Eventually, Jews were exterminated in a massive genocide called the "Final Solution." By the time Germany surrendered in May 1945, the Nazis were responsible for the murders of more than 6 million Jewish men, women, and children, as well as millions of other innocent people.

Many Jewish scientists had left Germany after the Nazis rose to power. With persecution growing worse and war growing more imminent, scientists in fascist nations fled to England, Scandinavia, and the United States. Otto Frisch left Germany in 1933 when Hitler became chancellor. Lise Meitner fled Germany for Sweden when Austria was annexed in 1938. But Werner Heisenberg, who continued to be one of Germany's most prominent scientists, refused to emigrate despite many pleas from his colleagues to join them. During World War II, he would serve as director of Germany's atomic bomb research project.

Werner Heisenberg (Atomic Archive)

Leo Szilard (Atomic Archive)

Nuclear fission became a source of great concern to refugee physicists such as Enrico Fermi, an Italian, and Leo Szilard, a Hungarian, who had both gone to live in the United States. They were fully aware of the potential of fission. Szilard feared the Germans were already developing an atom bomb. Knowing that Hitler would have no compunction about using such a weapon, Szilard wanted to keep all information about uranium fission secret, to slow down Germany's research. He writes in his memoirs:

> At that time it was already clear . . . that we were at the threshold of another world war. And so it seemed to us urgent to set up experiments which would show whether in fact neutrons are emitted in the fission process of uranium. I thought that if neutrons are in fact emitted in fission, this fact should be kept secret from the Germans.

Not all of Szilard's colleagues agreed with his view on the need for secrecy, however, and some papers discussing uranium fission experiments were published in the early 1940s.

Szilard began lobbying the United States government to begin a nuclear research program and recruited two other Hungarian scientists, Edward Teller and Eugene Wigner, to help him. But the trio, known as "the Hungarian conspiracy," had little success convincing the government of the seriousness of the threat.

Szilard enlisted the help of his old friend Albert Einstein, one of the most respected scientists in the world. Einstein agreed to do anything he could to warn of the dangers of nuclear weapons.

Einstein first agreed to write a letter to the Belgian government, since its colony, the Belgian Congo (the present-day Democratic Republic of the Congo), was the largest source of uranium. But upon

Edward Teller (Lawrence Livermore National Laboratory)

Albert Einstein regretted writing the letter to President Roosevelt persuading him to initiate an atomic bomb research project. (Library of Congress)

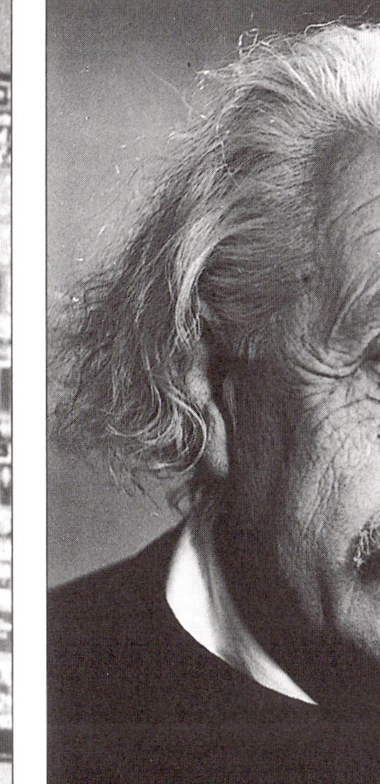

further thought, it was decided that they should approach President Roosevelt himself.

Szilard and Teller drove out to Einstein's vacation home on Long Island on July 30, 1939, and were greeted at the door by Einstein wearing a ratty old bathrobe and slippers. Szilard wrote about his meeting with Einstein years later.

> [Einstein] was willing to assume responsibility for sounding the alarm even though it was quite possible that the alarm might prove to be a false alarm. The one thing most scientists are really afraid of is to make fools of themselves. Einstein was free from such a fear . . .

Einstein dictated to Teller a draft of a letter to Roosevelt. The letter advised Roosevelt of the dangers of nuclear weapons and urged him to begin a nuclear research program in the United States. Einstein warned Roosevelt:

> This new phenomenon would also lead to the construction of bombs, and it is conceivable—though much less certain—that extremely powerful bombs of a new type, may thus be constructed. A single bomb of this type, carried by boat and exploded in a port, might very well destroy the whole port together with some of the surrounding territory.

Economist Alexander Sachs, an acquaintance of Szilard and unofficial adviser to Roosevelt, promised to personally deliver the letter to the president.

Szilard was right about Einstein's influence. Roosevelt wrote back to Einstein on October 19. Believing that the United States could not take the risk of allowing Hitler possession of "extremely powerful bombs," Roosevelt appointed the Advisory Committee on Uranium in

October 1939 to manage a federally funded uranium research program. Funding, however, was not made available until late 1940. This was the beginning of what would come to be known as the Manhattan Project.

Although war had broken out in Europe in September 1939, the committee did little to develop a serious research program, despite pleas from Szilard and his colleagues. The committee chairman, Lyman J. Briggs, distrusted the foreign scientists, believing they were trying to coax the United States into a European war. Briggs represented the prevailing isolationist sentiment among Americans, who, for the most part, wanted to stay out of the conflict, believing it was not their war. Also, nonscientists did not understand the concept of an atomic bomb. There appeared to be no reason compelling enough to warrant the time and money required to implement a rush program to develop a weapon that might not ever be used and might not work.

By the end of 1940, however, the entry of the United States into the war seemed inevitable. Germany had conquered much of Europe, including Belgium, which gave Germany control of one of the largest uranium deposits in the world. Uranium was a key component in nuclear weapons research.

The only thing saving Britain from the fate of so many other European countries was Germany's inability to launch an invasion across the English Channel. The British government considered setting up an atomic bomb program in Canada, where it would be safe from German air attacks, but Britain's resources were stretched to the limit fighting off the Germans. If an atomic bomb were to be developed outside of Germany, the United States would have to do it.

Two
Dangerous Science

We felt that neither the good nor the evil applications were our responsibility.
—James Franck, Manhattan Project physicist

In 1914 H. G. Wells, the English science-fiction author, published *The World Set Free,* a novel in which he prophesied a process of "nuclear disintegration" that unleashed "limitless power" and led to global nuclear war. Wells wrote of a worldwide conflict that left two hundred cities lying in utter ruin by the "unquenchable crimson conflagrations of the atomic bombs." Not even Wells could predict that his prophecies would so quickly be realized. Within twenty-five years, the first key steps had been taken that would turn science fiction into reality.

Hahn and Strassmann's groundbreaking 1938 experiments in atom splitting followed many other discoveries by scientists during the 1920s and early 1930s. As early as 1922, Niels Bohr, a Danish physicist known as the Great Dane to his colleagues, had published his theory of atomic structure, suggesting that each atom consists of a nucleus with electrons orbiting around it. In 1929 American physicist Ernest O. Lawrence conceived the idea for the first cyclotron, a machine better known as an "atom smasher." In 1932 British physicist James Chadwick had proven

H. G. Wells, the British science-fiction author, predicted the coming of atomic weapons in his novel The World Set Free, *published in 1914. (Library of Congress)*

the existence of neutrons. A year later French physicist Irène Joliot-Curie, the oldest daughter of Marie and Pierre Curie, and her husband, Frédéric Joliot, had discovered that radioactive elements could be produced from stable elements. This discovery of artificial radioactivity had far-reaching applications, particularly in medicine, but it also greatly advanced the development of nuclear weapons. All these discoveries contributed to the building of the first atomic bomb.

A key experiment that made the building of an atomic bomb feasible was conducted in extremely humble circumstances. In November 1940 the U.S. government appropriated forty thousand dollars to construct a system designed by Italian physicist Enrico Fermi to develop a self-sustaining chain reaction, the process that would prove to be the key to unleashing the power of the atom. The system relied on the use of uranium and graphite. The first choice for a site for the experiment was the Cook County Forest Preserve, southwest of Chicago. When this location became unworkable, the squash court beneath the University of Chicago's Stagg Field was chosen as an alternative. Although other experiments had already been conducted at the site, this particular experiment was totally unpredictable and very dangerous. Fermi was convinced that the chain reaction could be controlled and posed no danger except to the people actually carrying out the experiment, but scientists were risking a disaster by setting off a chain reaction in a crowded city.

The cyclotron, the world's most powerful "atom smasher" at the time, at the University of California Radiation Laboratory, Berkeley, in August 1939 (National Archives)

The experiment was performed on December 2, 1942. The center of the experiment consisted of an atomic pile—a five-hundred-ton pile of graphite bricks stacked in fifty-seven layers into which cubes of uranium and uranium oxide were embedded. Long control rods plated with an element called cadmium were set up so that they could be inserted into holes in the graphite bricks and withdrawn as required. The graphite would slow down the neutrons emitted by the uranium, and the cadmium in the rods would absorb them. As the control rods were withdrawn, fewer of the neutrons from the uranium would be absorbed, resulting in more split atoms—greater fission. The fission would produce neutrons faster than the cadmium could absorb them, a self-sustaining chain reaction, the action needed for the atomic bomb to work.

On that bitterly cold day, forty project scientists crammed onto the balcony overlooking the squash court to witness the experiment. Dust from the graphite filled the air and coated the floor. On a platform above the pile stood the "suicide squad," three young physicists holding buckets filled with cadmium salt. Their job was to douse the atomic pile if the experiment went out of control. On the floor with the atomic pile was George Weil, who was responsible for pulling the last control rod out of the pile. A second backup safety rod hung suspended from the balcony, and a project scientist stood ready with an ax to chop the rope so that the rod would drop into the pile and also theoretically stop the chain reaction. As the experiment began, Fermi shouted instructions to Weil from the crowded balcony.

At 10:37 A.M., Fermi told Weil to begin removing the last cadmium rod. The neutron counters began to click. Fermi took out his slide rule and carefully calculated the rate of increase in neutrons. Satisfied, he instructed Weil to remove the rod another six inches. The clicking on the neutron counter increased again. Calling out the neutron counts was Leona Woods, one of the few female scientists who worked on the project. Fermi did more calculations on his slide rule and seemed pleased with the results. The process continued for about an hour when there was suddenly a loud crash. The safety rod had released automatically, but it was unexpected because the pile was still subcritical. There was an insufficient mass of fissionable material to create a chain reaction. Unfazed, Fermi announced he was hungry, and told everyone to go to lunch.

A painting by Gary Sheehan depicting the world's first nuclear chain reaction conducted on a squash court at Stagg Field, University of Chicago, December 2, 1942 (National Archives)

Atomic physicists (left to right) Ernest O. Lawrence, Enrico Fermi, and Isidor Rabi (National Archives)

The experiment resumed at 2:00 that afternoon. Fermi instructed Weil to pull the control rod out another twelve inches. The neutron intensity increased more and more rapidly. Fermi raised his hand and announced, "The pile has gone critical." It was 3:53 P.M. when the first controlled release of energy from atomic nuclei occurred. A self-sustaining chain reaction was demonstrated beyond any doubt.

Not everyone was happy with the outcome of the experiment. Szilard had been instrumental in bringing this moment about, and he watched it happen from the balcony. He waited until everyone but Fermi had left. He later wrote, "I shook hands with Fermi and I said I thought this day would go down as a black day in the history of mankind."

Three
The Manhattan Project

I made one great mistake in my life—when I signed the letter to President Roosevelt recommending that an atomic bomb be made.
—Albert Einstein, Physicist

With the United States' entry into World War II, nuclear research became a top priority. By the summer of 1942, research had advanced far enough to make a full-scale bomb program feasible. In June 1942 President Roosevelt authorized the formation of the Manhattan Engineer District by the U.S. Army Corps of Engineers. This top-secret program came to be known as the Manhattan Project. Chosen to command the project was forty-six-year-old Colonel Leslie Richard Groves. Nicknamed "Greasy" when he was a cadet at West Point, Groves was a paunchy, five-foot-eleven-inch desk officer in the Corps of Engineers with a small mustache and weak handshake. Appointed to the provisional rank of colonel only since the outbreak of war, Groves had just finished supervising the construction of the Pentagon in Washington, D.C. He had a reputation for getting complex projects done on time and within budget. Groves knew how to cut through the miles of bureaucratic red tape that came with multimillion-dollar construction projects and, more important, he knew how to mold by-the-book military

General Leslie R. "Greasy" Groves, military director of the Manhattan Project (U.S. Department of Energy)

officers and clock-watching, sloppy civilians into a smoothly functioning team.

Groves had been hoping for an overseas combat assignment. Instead, his commanding officer informed him that the secretary of war had personally selected him for this very important position. At first Groves was totally unimpressed with the bomb project, though he reluctantly accepted command. Directing the Manhattan Project would be the most challenging mission of his career, but when he was assigned to it in 1942, Groves described himself as "probably the angriest officer in the United States Army."

The son of an army chaplain and a graduate of West Point, Groves was a career army officer through and through. An officer serving under him described Groves as:

> [T]he biggest sonavabitch I've ever met in my life, but also one of the most capable individuals. . . . He had absolute confidence in his decisions and he was absolutely ruthless in how he approached a problem to

> get it done. . . . I've often thought that if I were to have to do my part over again, I would select Groves as boss. I hated his guts and so did everybody else but we had our form of understanding.

When it came to accomplishing objectives, Groves was single-minded and totally distrustful of anyone who did not see things his way. He spied on people he distrusted, even going so far as to read their private mail. He delighted in bullying and humiliating people. Despite his shortcomings, Groves proved himself to be the best man for the job. Within days of his appointment, he quickly and efficiently solved problems that had lingered for months. On September 23, he was promoted to brigadier general.

The first order of business for Groves was to find a respected scientist to supervise the scientific side of the project. He did not understand the science behind the atomic bomb, and he knew the only way for the project to be successful was to give someone who did understand the science as much authority as Groves himself.

His first choice for the job was Ernest O. Lawrence, who had a reputation for being hardworking and practical. Lawrence, however, was already engaged in work essential to the war effort. After rejecting several other candidates, Groves focused on thirty-eight-year-old Dr. J. Robert Oppenheimer. Tall and thin with striking blue eyes and wild, bushy hair, Oppenheimer looked and acted like the eccentric genius he was. Chain-smoking and constantly flicking his nicotine-stained fingers were just two of Oppenheimer's many nervous habits. Known as "Oppie" to colleagues and friends, Oppenheimer was a New York City native who was already working on the bomb project. While acknowledged by peers as one of the most brilliant and versatile

J. Robert Oppenheimer, "Father of the Atomic Bomb" (U.S. Department of Energy)

nuclear physicists of his day, Oppenheimer had not won a Nobel Prize, even though some scientists working under him had. Although *Time* magazine would later dub Oppenheimer "Father of the Atomic Bomb," he had a reputation for being a sloppy scientist, clumsy in performing experiments and lacking the discipline needed to apply himself to a single problem long enough to accomplish Nobel Prize–quality work.

Oppenheimer seemed oblivious to all but his work and family. He read no magazines or newspapers, owned no radio, and showed no interest in politics. He had not learned of the disastrous stock market crash of 1929 until long after it happened. In 1936 Oppenheimer voted for the first time in a presidential election and began to take a closer look at the world around him. Appalled by the treatment of Jews in Germany, he began to understand how deeply economic and political events affected people's lives. While at the University of California in Berkeley,

Oppenheimer attended a few Communist Party meetings. He sympathized with many of the party's goals, but could not accept their dogma. Although he never joined the party, Oppenheimer's flirtations with it would come back to haunt him years later.

In Oppenheimer, Groves saw a man temperamentally fit for the job. Oppenheimer understood the egos and prejudices of the scientists, could sympathize with their attitudes and eccentricities, and could act as a filter between them and the military. Groves's appointment of Oppenheimer as scientific director of the Manhattan Project was greeted with astonishment by fellow scientists, who felt the project required a practical, hands-on scientist, not a theoretical physicist. The position also required a strong administrator, but Oppenheimer had never administered anything. Instead he'd gone from one university to another, doing work that he found interesting.

He and Groves were opposites in every respect. Groves was an "army brat" and the son of a stern, no-nonsense Presbyterian chaplain. Oppenheimer came from a wealthy, privileged, nonreligious Jewish family. His father was a successful businessman, and Oppenheimer had been educated at top schools and universities in New York City and Europe. He was insatiably curious about a wide range of subjects. One of his passions was Hindu philosophy. Oppenheimer taught himself the ancient language Sanskrit so that he could study sacred Hindu texts in their original language. Groves was not an intellectual, nor did he pretend to be one. He was an intensely practical man. He distrusted Oppenheimer on a personal level because of their differences, but he recognized the scientist's genius. After the war, Groves said in an interview:

> He's a genius. A real genius. While Lawrence is very bright he's not a genius, just a good hard worker. Why, Oppenheimer knows about everything. He can talk to you about anything you bring up. Well not exactly. I guess there are a few things he doesn't know about. He doesn't know anything about sports.

Despite their dissimilar personalities, Groves genuinely liked Oppenheimer and respected his ambition. Oppenheimer desperately wanted to direct the project and would do anything necessary to make it succeed. Those who initially questioned Oppenheimer's leadership abilities would later admit that he was the best man for the job. Commenting on Oppenheimer's appointment, physicist Isidor I. Rabi said it "was a real stroke of genius on the part of General Groves, who was not generally considered to be a genius." Groves and Oppenheimer did share some characteristics. Like Groves, Oppenheimer had a tremendous ego and great self-confidence. Although not the deliberate bully Groves was, Oppenheimer frequently offended people with his blunt criticisms and cutting sarcasm.

Immediately following his appointment, Oppenheimer proposed reorganizing the Manhattan Project scientists. Up till then they were scattered about the country working in different laboratories. Morale among the scientists was extremely low, and communication among them was terrible. Security was also a great concern, especially to Groves, for whom it was an absolute obsession. Oppenheimer proposed unifying the project, beginning with the establishment of a central laboratory under a single director where the bomb would be built. He suggested building the laboratory in an isolated area where scientists could work freely together in a secure environment.

Groves was delighted with Oppenheimer's proposal because he was thinking along the same lines. The first order of business was to choose a site for the central laboratory. This site would be the most secret of the entire Manhattan Project. Isolation was the top priority in choosing a site, but there were many other factors to consider also. The area had to be large enough to provide an adequate testing ground for the weapon. The climate had to be warm enough so that outdoor work could carry on through the winter. Access to the site by road and railroad was essential for bringing in massive amounts of material and large numbers of personnel. Sources of construction materials had to be close enough to keep costs reasonable. The population within a hundred-mile radius of the site had to be sparse in the interests of both safety and security. The location of the site also had to be remote from all seacoasts because of possible enemy attack. Several areas in the southwestern United States

Technical area map of Los Alamos

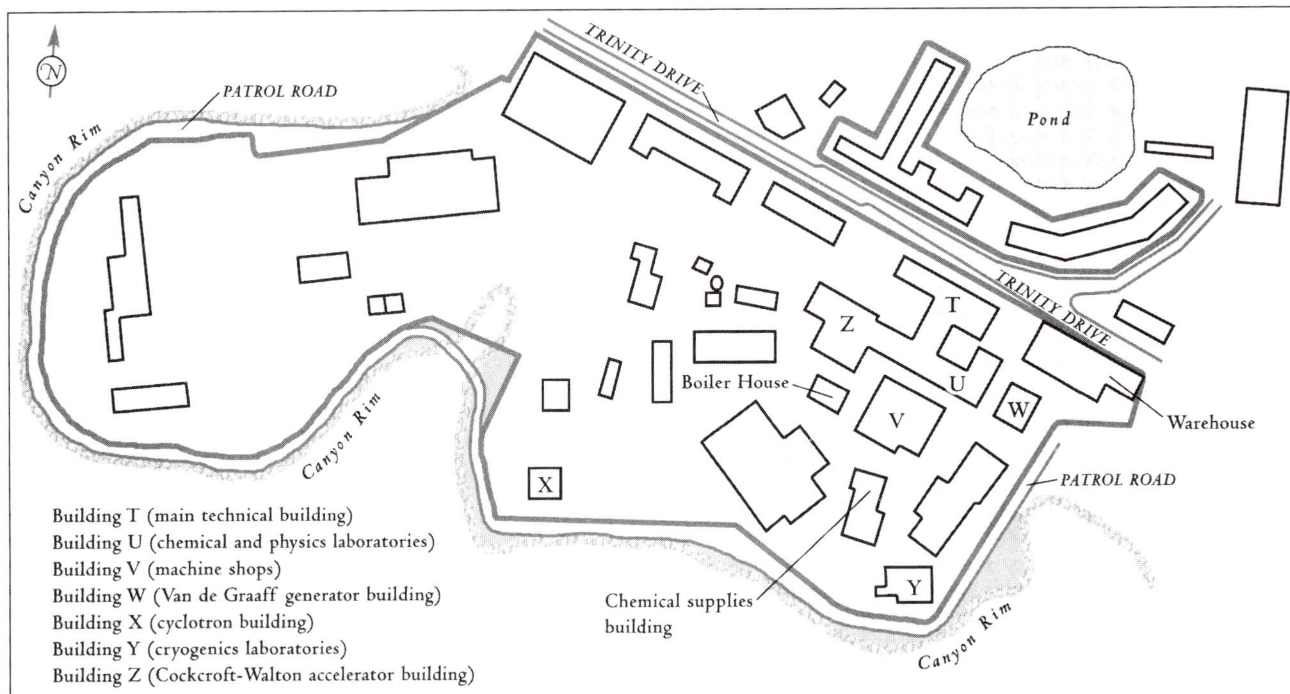

were considered, including Las Vegas, but a site in the vicinity of the Los Alamos Ranch School in New Mexico was chosen.

Oppenheimer had had this site in mind all along. He owned a vacation home nearby and knew that the isolation of the place was perfect for their purposes. A boarding school for boys had been located there, and the school's buildings could provide immediate housing for the project scientists. The site was also about thirty-five miles from Santa Fe, capital of New Mexico, which would be convenient for bringing in supplies. The federal government paid $440,000 for nine thousand acres of land at Los Alamos. Officially designated Site Y, no one referred to the installation as Los Alamos because the very name was deemed classified information. Most residents of Los Alamos and Santa Fe simply called it the Hill.

Surrounded by barbed wire in the middle of the desert, Site Y was where the actual design and construction of the two atomic bombs that would later be called "Fat Man" and "Little Boy" took place. These bombs were constructed using materials obtained from two other locations: Site X, in rural East Tennessee in an area then known as Black Oak Ridge; and Site W, in Hanford, Washington, on the Columbia River.

General Groves personally selected Black Oak Ridge as the location of Site X. Set in the Clinch River valley in the foothills of the Appalachian Mountains, the isolation of the area would minimize public awareness of the project's existence. The site was far enough inland and far enough away from densely populated areas to keep it relatively safe from enemy attack. It was also unclear what potential health hazards the plants to be built there would pose to local populations. The site had to be as far from populous areas as possible, and the terrain of the region created enough natural boundaries to minimize such dangers.

The Tennessee Valley Authority had huge hydroelectric plants in nearby Norris Dam and Watts Bar, which could supply the plants with the energy needed to operate. During the peak years of its operation, Site X consumed one-seventh of the total electrical output of the United States.

Unbeknownst to Groves was a prophecy foretold by a Tennessee mountain man named John Hendrix at the turn of the twentieth century. Legend has it that one night Hendrix was lying on the ground, looking at the sky near his home in the woods on Pine Ridge. A voice told him to go into the wilderness and stay there for forty days and forty nights in meditation and prayer. Hendrix returned with an extraordinary vision of the future.

> Bear Creek Valley some day will fill with great buildings and factories and they will help win the greatest war that will ever be.
>
> There will be a city on Black Oak Ridge and I say the center of authority will be middleway between Tadlock's farm and Pyatt's Place.
>
> A railroad will spur off the main L&N, run down toward Robertsville and then branch off toward Scarbrough. It will serve the great city of my vision. This I know.
>
> Big engines will dig big ditches. . . . Thousands of people will run to and fro. They will build things and there will be great noise and confusion and the earth will shake.
>
> I've seen it. It's comin'.

Hendrix's neighbors thought his strange vision was due to drinking too much whiskey, or to insanity. No one knows for sure when he made these predictions, but people who knew Hendrix remember him speaking of his vision of the secret city as early as 1901, more than forty years before it was built.

A. L. Robinette, an Oak Ridge farmer, was one of the many people displaced by the government when it claimed land to build the Manhattan Project sites. (U.S. Department of Energy)

Vision or myth, the site at Black Oak Ridge was begun by the U.S. government in the fall of 1942 when fifty-six thousand acres were purchased in Anderson and Roane counties in Tennessee. Within this tract were several small farming communities, and the families living in them had been there for generations. These people were forced to leave their homes and livelihood for the sake of the war effort. Some went willingly, believing they were doing their patriotic duty in a time of crisis. But others were very bitter about having to leave land that had been in their families for generations. Although they were paid for their property (and there is debate to this day about the fairness of that compensation), they resented being forced to give up something in which they had invested so much of their lives, and which also had a history and legacy that were priceless.

The government gave these families little warning about their eviction and did little to assist them with relocation. If they refused to sell their homes, the government would take them anyway and evict the residents by force. The Corps of Engineers tried to allow six weeks for evacuation, but many residents were given only two. One displaced landowner recalled after the war:

> All the folks in these parts were farmers. They worked the ground and minded their own business, peaceful folks living a simple life. We didn't pay much attention to the outside world and they didn't bother with us. That was up to 1942, anyway, when one day a man came to our house and said he was from the Government. "We're going to buy up your land," he said to me. "All of it?" I asked. "Yes sir," he said, "we're going to buy all the land in this section. Everyone has to go."

The Corps of Engineers had the monumental task of building from scratch four massive industrial complexes and a residential community

Technical area map of Clinton Engineer Works (U.S. Department of Energy)

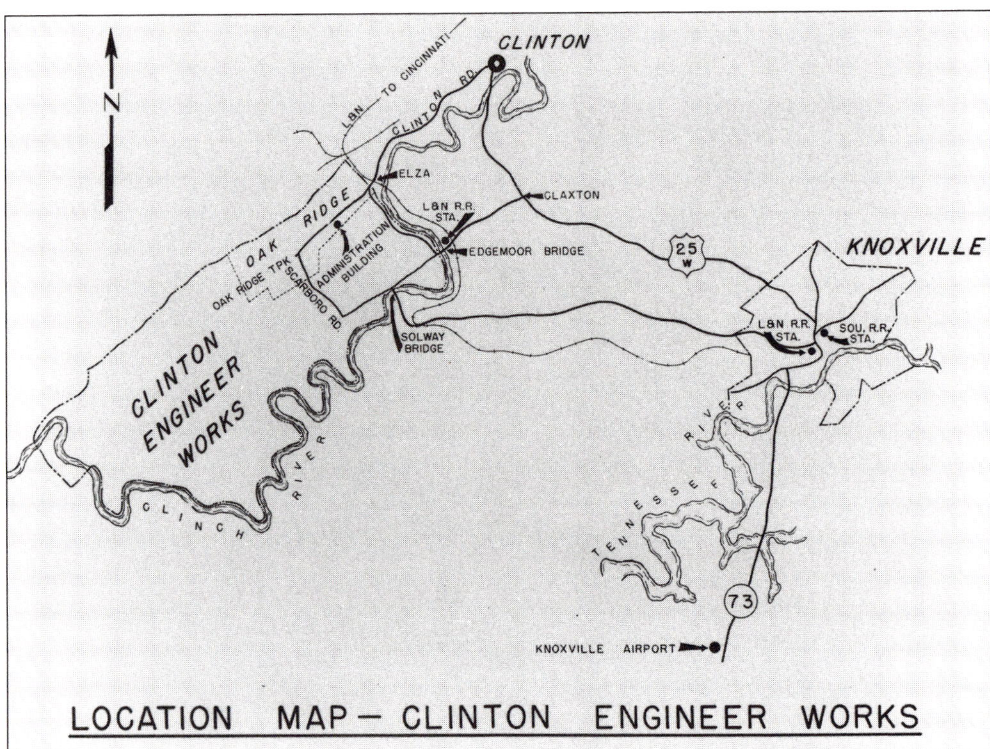

for all of the people working on the project. In addition, three hundred miles of road and fifty-five miles of railroad track were needed. All of this construction had to be completed within just a few months.

The site was first code-named the Kingston Demolition Range, for a nearby town in Roane County. In early 1943 the name was changed to the more innocuous Clinton Engineer Works, named for the neighboring county seat of Anderson County, and was referred to as CEW. The site retained that official designation for the duration of the war, but it came to be called Oak Ridge by those who lived and worked there. The Oak Ridge site would be responsible for producing the type of uranium, U-235, that would be used for the Manhattan Project. Four plants were built there: K-25, S-50, Y-12, and X-10. The four plants operating at the same time consumed 20 percent more electricity than all of New York City.

The Manhattan Project needed a third site that could accommodate full-scale plutonium production facilities. There was not enough power to support that kind of major facility in Oak Ridge, and the site was too close to a major city, Knoxville, Tennessee. In the event of a major catastrophe involving plutonium, all its people would be in danger. After surveying several places in California, Oregon, and Washington, Groves's staff agreed that a 500,000-acre area located on arid tableland between a bend in the Columbia River and Rattlesnake Mountain near Hanford, Washington, best met the criteria for the plutonium production site. The Grand Coulee and Bonneville dams would provide sufficient hydroelectric power, and the flat but rocky terrain offered an excellent foundation for the massive plutonium plants to be constructed. The site was far enough inland to meet security requirements, and existing roadways and transportation facilities could be quickly improved. Groves authorized the establishment of the Hanford Engineer Works (HEW), code-named Site W.

The land acquired by the Corps of Engineers included three communities, each home to approximately three hundred residents. Another two hundred people lived thirty miles downriver in Richland. In addition, one thousand farmers and ranchers had a stake in fifty thousand acres of farmland, mostly irrigated fruit orchards. Just as in Oak Ridge, the people in these communities faced eviction from their homes. Former Hanford resident Annette Heriford remembers the high price she and her neighbors paid to accommodate the Manhattan Project.

> In March 1943, when I was about 22, we received a letter from the government saying that we would have to move in 30 days. It was a terrible shock. I can't describe it. It was unbelievable. The only thing that made it credible to us was because of the war. Our town had been chosen for the war effort. We were so patriotic . . . it was still a terrible blow. . . . In spite of our patriotism, I remember one man stood there with a shotgun and said they would have to move him.

The people forced to leave did not know the reason for their eviction. The Manhattan Project was top secret.

The Corps of Engineers immediately set to work constructing a sprawling industrial complex to manufacture plutonium. There were seven separate processing units—three reactors, three chemical-separation plants, and one fuel-fabrication facility. Since fuel fabrication was the unit least likely to cause a serious accident, it was constructed about seven miles away from the population center in Richland. The reactors, consid-

Enrico Fermi directed the experiment leading to the world's first nuclear chain reaction on a squash court at the University of Chicago. He had received the Nobel Prize for Physics in 1938. (National Archives)

ered to be the most potentially dangerous facilities, were built farthest away from the town.

Another important branch of the Manhattan Project was the Metallurgical Laboratory at the University of Chicago. Known as the Met Lab, it had played a critical role in developing breakthrough technologies in the years leading up to the formation of the official Manhattan Project. Fermi conducted the historic chain reaction there, and Glenn Seaborg would later carry out vital experiments on plutonium separation and concentration. Although the role of Met Lab would change to that of a supporting laboratory as the other project sites became operational, physicists such as James Franck, Leo Szilard, Eugene Wigner, and Walter

Glenn Seaborg discovered plutonium with Edwin McMillan. (Atomic Archive)

Zinn would continue important theoretical studies there and at other institutions such as California Institute of Technology, Columbia University in New York, and the University of California, Berkeley.

The race was on. Driven by the fear that Nazi Germany could produce an atomic weapon at any moment, thousands of people worked twenty-four hours a day, seven days a week in a massive top-secret enterprise with one goal—to beat the Germans by building it first. The fate of the world was at stake.

Four
Secret Cities, Secret Lives

The Manhattan Engineer District bore no relation to the industrial or social life of our country; it was a separate state, with its own airplanes and its own factories and its thousands of secrets. It had a peculiar sovereignty, one that could bring about the end, peacefully or violently, of all other sovereignties.
—HERBERT S. MARKS, GENERAL COUNSEL FOR THE ATOMIC ENERGY COMMISSION

Thousands of workers were needed to operate the massive secret industrial complexes in Hanford, Los Alamos, and Oak Ridge. Since the project was so secret, the Corps of Engineers had to build entire secret cities where these workers could be isolated in self-contained communities that included churches, hospitals, schools, recreation centers, and stores.

Housing shortages at project sites were a constant problem. Requirements were always underestimated. The army needed to attract and keep personnel who were essential to the project, such as engineers, scientists, and technicians. Creating a relatively attractive and comfortable living environment would make those essential personnel more likely to stay with the project for the duration. The army realized that people would be much happier in their work if they had their families close to them, so the towns were built to support young families with children.

In Oak Ridge, a largely successful effort was made to preserve the natural contours of the land; groups of houses were clustered in neighborhoods, each with its own elementary school and small shopping center. Close to these neighborhoods was a central business district, a dental clinic, a hospital, a library, and the town's one high school. Two chapels and several recreation centers and cafeterias also were built in the area. By 1945 Oak Ridge had 165 businesses, including 13 groceries, 9 drugstores, 7 movie theaters, a department store, and 17 restaurants.

The homes originally built in Oak Ridge were called "Cemesto houses" because they were constructed out of a prefabricated material that was a composite of cement and asbestos. Houses were built in a variety of sizes and designated by a letter. A- and B-houses were small, two-bedroom homes. C-houses had a third bedroom, and D-houses had a separate dining room. Larger F-, G-, and H-houses were built later for top project officials. Every house had a picture window in the living room, a fireplace, and hardwood floors. They were all equipped with refrigerators and stoves and heated by coal furnaces. Although not built

The B-house was a small but cozy two-bedroom housing unit. (U.S. Department of Energy)

The spacious D-house, which had three bedrooms and a separate dining room, was allocated to only the most elite members of the Manhattan Project. (U.S. Department of Energy)

for longevity, many of these houses still stand, remodeled and home to hundreds of Oak Ridge families.

Street names in the town were designated systematically. Avenues, running east to west, were given names of states and proceeded alphabetically. Circles, lanes, and roads leading from the avenues were given names beginning with the first letter of the name of the avenue. The military arranged the streets this way to simplify record keeping for maintenance and for reporting crimes and fires. It was also easier for residents to find their way around town.

As the demands of the project grew, the army had to keep changing its estimates of the town's ultimate size. In the first, main phase of construction, the army called for a city of twelve thousand people with a thoughtfully planned community comprising three neighborhoods, a high school, and a business district. The plan quickly became obsolete as expansion of the plants created a demand for more workers and housing. The second phase, begun in the fall of 1943, called for a town of forty-two thousand residents. A year later, the population swelled to sixty-six thousand. By the time "Little Boy" was dropped on Hiroshima, the population of Oak Ridge exceeded seventy-five thousand. At that time, Oak Ridge was the fifth largest city in Tennessee, but very few outsiders had ever visited it or knew of its existence.

When production began at Hanford in 1943, housing was constructed to accommodate six thousand operations workers and eleven thousand family members. By early 1945 there were 4,304 new housing units, along with churches, medical facilities, schools, and shops. There were 2,500 conventional wood-frame houses that came in different styles, from two-bedroom one-story duplexes to four-bedroom two-story family homes. In addition, there were 1,800 small, prefabricated houses shipped in from Portland, Oregon.

Only qualified people could live in a house at the project sites. Having a family did not automatically entitle you to a house; eligibility was determined by job. Scientists, specialized technicians, and military officers were always at the top of the list for good housing. At Los Alamos, the most prized houses were in a neighborhood called Bathtub Row. These log houses, once part of the Ranch School, were the only homes with bathtubs. The rest of the houses had showers. Top scientists were given the houses on Bathtub Row. The more specialized someone's work was and the more essential that person was to the project, the better his

Women's dormitory at Los Alamos (MPHPA)

Trailers were not desirable housing, but they were better than hutments. (U.S. Department of Energy)

Trailer housing at Los Alamos (MPHPA)

or her house. Construction workers, general laborers, and less essential operational personnel had to settle for less comfortable housing.

After houses, the most desirable accommodations were apartments and dormitories. Other housing at the sites included barracks; trailer camps; hutments; and temporary, flimsily built units called "victory cottages" used for housing families. Hutments were the most spartan of the housing units at the project sites. These sixteen-square-foot plywood structures had no windows and only one door. Four people shared each tiny building. There was room for little more than a bed in each corner and a potbellied stove in the middle of the space. In the summer, if housing shortages were particularly acute, the stove was moved out to make room for a fifth bed. Families living in hutments occupied two buildings put together. Residents of hutments shared centrally located bathroom facilities.

Occupying many of these hutments were the thousands of African Americans who were recruited from all parts of the Deep South to work on the Manhattan Project. The majority of blacks worked as domestics,

Women hang wash on a clothesline outside their hutments. African Americans lived in segregated housing, usually in the least desirable places. (U.S. Department of Energy)

Even outhouse facilities were segregated in Oak Ridge. (U.S. Department of Energy)

Due to discriminatory practices of the time, African Americans such as these sanitation workers were relegated to unskilled labor at the Manhattan Project sites. (U.S. Department of Energy)

as janitors, or in other menial jobs. Few blacks were hired for skilled or technical jobs; nonetheless, most were making more money working for the Manhattan Project than they had ever made before. The original plans for Oak Ridge had called for a "Negro Village" to be built in the east part of town. Only African Americans would live there, but they would have housing, shopping facilities, a church, and even a school.

Towns throughout the southern United States at this time were segregated. Blacks had to live apart from whites, and Oak Ridge would be no exception. Segregation laws demanded that African-American children attend separate schools and they were almost always inferior. Blacks had to ride in the backs of buses and on separate cars in trains, and had to enter through the back doors of restaurants and theaters and sit in sections segregated from whites. They could not drink out of the same water fountains, use the same bathrooms, or stay in the same hotels as whites. The plan for the Negro Village at Oak Ridge was abandoned because of the demand for more housing for whites. African Americans

African-American teenagers had to use a segregated recreation hall for their dances in Oak Ridge. (U.S. Department of Energy)

had to live in hutments until 1950. Married couples were not allowed to live together. A five-foot-high fence topped with barbed wire separated men and women. Black children were not allowed to live in Oak Ridge until 1945.

Thousands of African Americans came to Hanford, too, attracted by high wages. They also lived in segregated housing, but other types of segregation were not as strict. Luzelle Johnson, a black laborer from Mobile, Alabama, recalls that blacks and whites at least ate together and played together. "I didn't run into much racism at Hanford," he recalls. "Everybody was working together, and everybody was eating together at the mess halls. White and colored could go in together and eat. . . . Everybody played baseball together."

The military recognized early on that in order for workers to be efficient and productive, they needed to be happy. The better the morale of the workers, the better their productivity and the quality of their work would be. People needed ways to help them cope with the oppres-

A large community swimming pool was one of the amenities the army used to make the Oak Ridge townsite appealing to families. (U.S. Department of Energy)

Theater at Los Alamos (MPHPA)

sive and stressful environment of the project sites. Recreation halls were built where workers could socialize. They played cards, listened to the jukebox, danced, or just relaxed. In addition to the recreation halls, there were various kinds of entertainment facilities, such as soda fountains, ice-skating rinks, and drive-in and indoor movie theaters.

Manhattan Project residents took it upon themselves to create their own cultural institutions. The first Oak Ridge Public Library was an old army ambulance painted to resemble a circus wagon. This traveling library, a kind of early bookmobile, visited residential areas so that people could borrow books. Los Alamos also established a public library.

In 1943 Oak Ridge's first newspaper, the *Oak Ridge Journal*, was established. It featured social columns, such as church announcements, movie reviews, schedules of community events, and neighborhood news. The newspaper was delivered by horseback before a postal service was established. An Oak Ridge scientist organized a symphony orchestra made up of scientists, technicians, and servicemen. Los Alamos organized a choral group. At each site, musicians formed bands, theater groups produced plays, and dances were held regularly on weekend evenings. Arts-and-crafts and hobby groups also were established. There was even a "closed-circuit" radio station at Los Alamos, Station KRS, which could only broadcast within the site. The station borrowed records from residents to play on the air, and local performers often shared their talents on the radio. At Hanford, sports were a popular form of recreation, especially baseball.

In their efforts to create a typical small-town atmosphere for workers and their families, army officials encouraged civilians to form civic,

Children check out books from the first Oak Ridge Public Library, an old army ambulance painted to resemble a circus wagon. (U.S. Department of Energy)

Baseball was a popular recreational activity at all of the Manhattan Project sites. This team is named the Army Bombers. (U.S. Department of Energy)

patriotic, and social clubs. They served as morale boosters and helped build a sense of community and identity. The army, of course, favored patriotic organizations such as the American Legion, Daughters of the American Revolution, and Veterans of Foreign Wars. They also encouraged fraternal orders such as the Masons by providing these groups with meeting space. Army officials had the absolute right to accept or reject any group. Oak Ridgers responded enthusiastically. By the end of the war, there were more than thirty fraternal, patriotic, professional, and social organizations on the Oak Ridge site.

Religion was important to many of the residents, who were free to organize religious congregations as they wished. By the end of the war, there were twenty-two separate congregations in Oak Ridge alone.

Oak Ridge children playing outside one of the recreational halls (U.S. Department of Energy)

Hanford Protestant Church, 1947 (U.S. Department of Energy)

In addition to satisfying the religious and recreational needs of workers, army officials recognized the importance of education and health. Comprehensive health-care programs were developed, and clinics and hospitals were constructed. Physicians made house calls, and regular sanitary inspections of cafeterias, dorms, and other public areas were implemented. Army officials also had to offer potential employees excellent schools as an incentive to join the project. Until Oak Ridge schools were integrated in 1955, younger black children attended a segregated school at the site, but high school students were bused to nearby Knoxville.

After-school and weekend activities for children were limited. Initially one of the only things to do was to go to the movies. When there was an increase in juvenile delinquency, the army opened recreation cen-

Social activities were organized for teenagers, such as this dance held in an Oak Ridge recreation hall. (U.S. Department of Energy)

ters for school-age children and teens. Dances were occasionally organized for teenagers. The army allowed participation in local branches of the Boy Scouts and Girl Scouts, but there were no adults on the project sites trained to lead groups of young people in recreational activities.

Most residents relied on public transportation to get around. At the central terminal in Oak Ridge, there were three kinds of buses: off-area, which ran between Oak Ridge and other towns and cities such as Chattanooga and Knoxville; area buses, which transported people between commercial and residential areas on the site itself; and work buses, which took people to work at the plants. What many Oak Ridgers remember most vividly about the central terminal was a

Brownie Scouts sitting outside at Elm Grove School in Oak Ridge. The army encouraged the Manhattan Project sites to have organized activities for young people, such as Boy Scouts and Girl Scouts. (U.S. Department of Energy)

The Oak Ridge High School Prom (U.S. Department of Energy)

The Central Bus Terminal in Oak Ridge. Workers had to ride a bus from their townsite to the plant at which they worked. (U.S. Department of Energy)

constant "atmosphere of rudeness and hurry." Oak Ridgers who were otherwise polite apparently resorted to pushing and shoving in the mad commuter rushes at the bus terminal.

The army went to extraordinary lengths to make everyday life as comfortable as possible for people, but residents still had plenty of things

Oak Ridgers wait in line to go shopping for groceries at the A&P. Waiting in long lines for just about everything was a constant nuisance. (U.S. Department of Energy)

to complain about. Having to stand in lines for food, entertainment, a seat on the bus, and even medical attention were frustrations every Oak Ridger had to endure. Mud was a problem at Oak Ridge and Los Alamos. Clearing the land to build the communities had destroyed much of the ground cover, resulting in pervasive mud. Wooden sidewalks were installed in Oak Ridge along commonly traveled routes, but they provided only minimal protection. An anonymous Oak Ridge resident wrote this about the mud:

In order not to check in late,
I've had to lose a lot of weight,
From swimming through a fair-sized flood
And wading through the goddam mud.

I've lost my rubbers and my shoes
Perpetually I have the blues
My spirits tumble with a thud
Because of all this goddam mud.

Mud was a constant problem in Oak Ridge. (U.S. Department of Energy)

It's in my system so that when
I cut my finger now and then
Instead of bleeding just plain blood
Out pours a stream of goddam mud!

Among residents at Site X, a common ailment was the "Oak Ridge croup," a persistent cough picked up from inhaling the red dust that was stirred up constantly by the buses transporting residents and workers. At Hanford, residents also had to contend with dust. Many of the people who came to Hanford expected to be moving to the Evergreen State, as Washington is better known, not to the desertlike place they found upon arriving. Windstorms frequently kicked up sand to the point that it was unbearable to be outdoors for even a short time. Robley Johnson, the Hanford site photographer, recalls that sometimes it was bad enough to make new workers quit: "A lot of them would get off the bus, stand around for a while, see a dust storm coming and get on the next bus back to Pasco. They never even stayed overnight, a lot of them." An anonymous Hanford resident wrote:

'Twas on a hot and dusty day
In August '43
I saw a cloud of Hanford dust
Blow high to welcome me.

Willie Daniels, a Hanford worker, remembers what it was like after one bad storm: "The next morning there was so much wind and so much dust, everything was plowed up, you could write your name on our luggage."

Dormitory residents had to contend with bedbugs, nasty little insects that inflict painful bites resulting in red welts on the body. One Oak Ridger recalls the campaign her husband waged to rid their dorm of bedbugs:

> He concocted a mixture of kerosene, gasoline, and Flit (an insecticide) and sprayed it all over the room. No crack escaped treatment. The mattress got particular attention, an all-day sunning with a thorough spraying, and all our clothes were aired on the clothes line. The campaign, to my relief, was a success.

Life in the trailers also had many hardships. A worker could not call the place his or her own because someone from a previous shift would have slept in it while he or she was working. Toilets were located in a central building, so those who had to go to the bathroom in the middle of the night kept their waste in the trailer in a "slop jar," and emptied it in the morning. Telephones were also in a central building, so names were announced over a loudspeaker for phone calls.

Crimes of varying degrees were committed at all the sites, but Hanford was plagued with the most. In many ways, the atmosphere in Hanford resembled that of a western frontier town; gambling and heavy drinking often led to fights and thefts. There were instances of serious crimes, such as sexual assaults and homicides, but they were rare. Breaking the law did not lead to automatic termination from Hanford. Workers were needed for the plants, so minor infractions were overlooked.

More than 140,000 civilians worked at the various locations of the Manhattan Project. Men made up the majority of these workers, but there were thousands of women who also made important contributions. Before World War II, women had been discouraged from working outside the home. The war, however, created a serious labor shortage as millions of men were drafted into military service. Women had to fill in. On the Manhattan Project they worked in a variety of jobs—as clerks, secretaries, plant workers, security officers, and even in some specialized

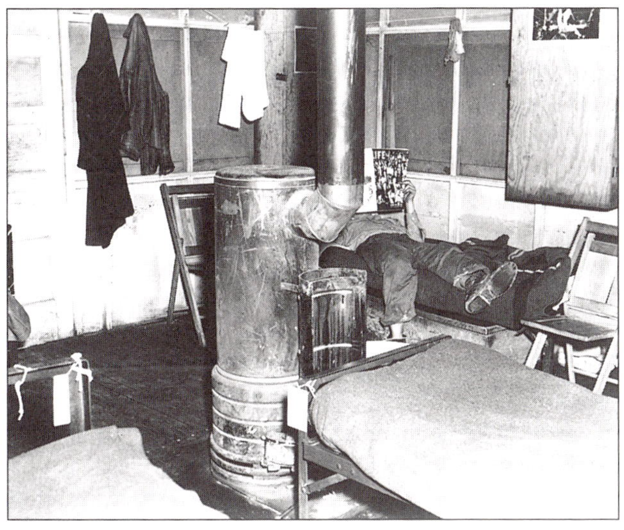

Hutments were the least desirable of Mahattan Project housing. As many as five people would have to share the sixteen-square-foot structures. (U.S. Department of Energy)

technical positions. They worked side by side with men, which was quite unusual for the time. In addition to civilian women workers, there was a 422-member Women's Army Corps (WAC) detachment assigned to the Manhattan Project. WACs were stationed at all the project sites and had a variety of duties, ranging from stenography and operating telephone switchboards to code writing and deciphering. WACs were assigned to handle records, technical reports, and other secret information considered too sensitive for civilian access.

Operators maintaining control room panels at the Y-12 plant in Oak Ridge. With so many men serving in the armed forces overseas, women filled many jobs that would normally have been men's. (U.S. Department of Energy)

Although African Americans and women did not hold the high-level positions considered crucial to the Manhattan Project, each made his or her own contributions. Everyone, from nuclear physicists to janitors, was essential to its ultimate success.

Workers leaving the Y-12 plant in Oak Ridge at the end of their shift (U.S. Department of Energy)

Five
Saboteurs and Spies

Maintaining security is always a losing battle in the end.
—General Leslie R. Groves, Manhattan Project Director

To live in any of the Manhattan Project sites during World War II was to live in an environment of tight security and total secrecy. Espionage and sabotage were constant concerns fueled by speculation about what progress the Germans were making with atomic research. The thousands of people who worked in the plants never knew exactly what they were developing. Through a security measure called "compartmentalization," workers knew only what they needed to know to perform their particular jobs. Every person living in Hanford, Los Alamos, and Oak Ridge, whether they worked for the project or not, had to wear an identification badge at all times within the gates. Putting on a badge became as natural as putting on underwear. Scientist Chris Keim remembers how much trouble workers would have if they did not wear their badges:

> We wore our badges all the time within the gates of Oak Ridge. . . . One day, as I was getting off a bus, I was grabbed by the MPs (military police) in the townsite. They took me aside and pointed to my badge. I was

> unaware of it, but my badge had been partially hidden by my turned-up overcoat collar. Wearing badges became such a habit . . . that I found myself showing my badge to the minister on Sunday mornings as I left church.

Plant workers' badges had roman numerals that indicated the amount of information they could receive. Roman numeral V was for top project officials; roman numeral I was for the lowest-level workers. Letters on the badges indicated in what part of the plant a person was employed, and his or her access was limited to that area.

No one was permitted to talk about the work at the plants to anyone, not even to spouses or children. New residents entering Oak Ridge received a bulletin that read: "You are now a resident of Oak Ridge, situated within a restricted military area. . . . What you do here, What you see here, What you hear here, let it stay here." The army imposed harsh penalties on anyone who talked to unauthorized persons or took information outside the workplace. Supervisors gave their employees daily warnings

Sign alerting visitors to Oak Ridge security zones (U.S. Department of Energy)

Workers punch a time clock before beginning their shifts at a plant. (U.S. Department of Energy)

Manhattan Project workers were reminded of strict security precautions everywhere they went. (U.S. Department of Energy)

about the importance of secrecy. Billboards, handbills, and posters reminding people to keep their work secret were posted all over the sites. Employees and residents had to endure constant surprise searches and checks by security personnel. Being fired was the worst thing that could happen to a resident. He or she lost not only a source of income, but also

All vehicles entering Manhattan Project sites were subjected to a thorough search by security officers. (U.S. Department of Energy)

housing. People who were fired were blacklisted by the military, so they would never again be eligible for government employment.

Security forces for the project sites were established when construction began on the plants. Armed guards were posted at the entry points. Everyone going into the communities was subject to a thorough search and intense scrutiny of his or her identification. Fencing was put in place at strategic points in exposed areas. Guards on horseback patrolled the natural boundaries of the perimeter. By 1945 Oak Ridge security forces included 4,900 civilian guards, 740 military policemen, and more than 400 civilian policemen. Hanford, Los Alamos, and Oak Ridge became cities behind fences.

To ensure security throughout the Manhattan Project, the military established a unit called the Intelligence and Security Division that operated with the cooperation and support of army intelligence and the

Federal Bureau of Investigation. The job of this unit was to anticipate potential espionage and sabotage situations. Among the division's operatives were 500 undercover agents, known as G-2s to the residents, who worked in civilian clothes posing as civilian residents and workers.

Vincent "Bud" Whitehead was one of these counterintelligence agents. Whitehead posed as an official photographer at Hanford. He carried a special pistol and drove an intercept car, a Ford that could go 102 miles an hour, fast for that time. In the car, Whitehead had a complete arsenal of weapons—a rifle, a machine gun, and a gas gun. He also flew a small plane over the Hanford site every morning to check the fencing. His main job was to spy on people at Hanford. "Everybody was spied upon," Whitehead recalls. "We did spot checks on telephone conversations. . . . The purpose was to find out who was breaking security." An agent posing as a plant employee might ride the bus and try to engage a real worker in conversation about his or her duties at the plant to test their loyalty.

Even Santa Claus had to submit to a thorough search by security officers before being allowed entry to Oak Ridge. (U.S. Department of Energy)

An Oak Ridge security officer surrounded by confiscated guns, cameras, and other restricted items (U.S. Department of Energy)

Another duty of the security agents was to record "un-Americanisms." Any criticism of or negative comments about President Roosevelt, the project, or the war could be recorded and possibly held against a person. People working for the Manhattan Project had to be willing to sacrifice many of their civil liberties, such as freedom of speech. Security agents also recruited project employees and residents to spy on one another. "I got calls at all times of the day and night," Whitehead recalls. "I told them they were working for the U.S. government, in a highly classified job. And not to tell anybody what they did because it might get them killed. I had two old ladies there in their sixties who were especially active." It is unknown how many civilian spies were recruited, but it is likely that there were many neighbors watching one another and reporting to the security forces anything they deemed suspicious. People believed that spying on their neighbors was helping the war effort.

Items in households such as binoculars, cameras, firearms, and telescopes had to be registered with the military. Death certificates and sympathy letters to outside relatives of employees who died on the project were designated classified documents and not delivered to the next of kin until after the war. At Los Alamos, the most secret of the project sites, security measures were even more extreme. All personal mail was subject to censorship. Letters had to be mailed in unsealed envelopes. Packages could not be sealed or tied until inspected by a security officer.

Most people in Hanford, Los Alamos, and Oak Ridge respected the extreme and oppressive security measures and went out of their way

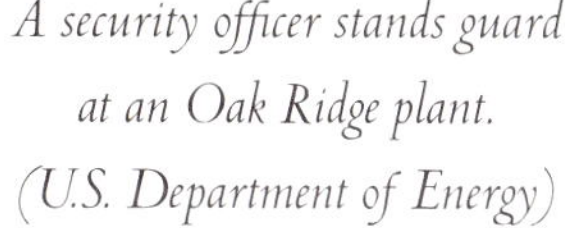

A security officer stands guard at an Oak Ridge plant. (U.S. Department of Energy)

to abide by them. They may have viewed them as a daily annoyance, but they believed that in a time of war such extraordinary measures were necessary. The necessity of these extensive security precautions is debatable. No acts of espionage or sabotage against the Hanford or Oak Ridge plants have been recorded, but it was discovered soon after Japan surrendered that Soviet spies had infiltrated Los Alamos.

In order to carry out successful atomic experiments, scientists had to discover a *moderator* in which to encase uranium and thus slow down the neutrons in the fission process. It was crucial that the moderator itself absorb few neutrons. Two primary candidates for effective moderators were carbon and a substance called "heavy water," which contains oxygen and a rare form of hydrogen called deuterium. Enrico Fermi and Herbert L. Anderson discovered that carbon would be a perfect moderator. Ordinarily the scientists would have published their findings, but they agreed not to for fear it might help the Germans build an atomic bomb. Fermi then went on to try graphite, a form of carbon, in the crucial 1942 experiment at the University of Chicago.

In the meantime, a German physicist named Walther Bothe experimented with an impure batch of carbon and came to the erroneous conclusion that carbon was an inadequate neutron moderator. Had he been able to read Fermi and Anderson's paper, Bothe would have seen where his findings went wrong. But the paper remained unpublished, and German scientists turned their focus on the difficult process of producing heavy water as a moderator.

After conquering Norway in 1940, Germany had come into possession of one of the only facilities in the world capable of producing heavy water in any quantity. Located in Vemork in southern Norway, the plant became an important target of Allied attacks. Following his appointment as head of the Manhattan Project, General Groves requested that action be taken against the plant. A British plan to destroy it was already under way. On October 19, 1942, an advance party of four Norwegian commandos parachuted into the area. They were to be followed the next month by two glider planes carrying demolition experts. Both gliders, crossing the North Sea from Scotland, crashed in Norway. The fourteen survivors were captured by the Germans and immediately executed.

The destruction of the plant was considered so vital that the British ordered another raid. For the next mission, on February 16, 1943, six specially trained Norwegians parachuted onto a frozen lake thirty miles away from the plant. They were able to rendezvous with the four Norwegians of the original advance party. One member of the party skied over to the plant to gather current information. Since the failed glider assault, plant security had been improved, but only fifteen soldiers guarded the facility because its natural barriers were considered impenetrable. One of the commandos wrote: "We understood how the Germans could allow themselves to keep so small a guard there. The colossus lay there like a medieval castle built in the most inaccessible place, protected by precipices and rivers."

On the evening of February 27, the commandos set out to attack the massive seven-story factory. They had the element of surprise and excellent intelligence on their side. A man involved in building part of the plant had escaped to Britain and was working for British intelligence. He identified a cable intake tunnel that bypassed most of the defenses and led directly to the heavy-water plant. Two commandos were able to crawl through the tunnel and leave an explosive in place without being detected by the Germans.

The operation was a success. No one on either side was killed or injured, but the heavy-water plant was temporarily crippled. The British estimated that it would be out of operation for at least a year, but shortly thereafter intercepted reports that maintained the Germans had mounted a major repair effort. Increased security at the plant made another commando raid impossible. Groves pushed for stronger action. On November 16, 1943, two hundred B-17 bombers, called Flying Fortresses, dropped four hundred tons of bombs on the plant and surrounding areas. The bombs were dropped from a high altitude, making accuracy very difficult, and only twelve of them actually hit the target. Despite the limited damage, it was enough to shut down the plant and convince the Germans it was pointless to put it back into operation because there was no way to effectively defend it from air attack.

The heavy-water plant was dismantled and sent to Germany. In February 1944 the last of the heavy water, about 1,323 pounds, was shipped on a ferry bound for Germany. The Allies learned of the shipment and informed the Norwegian underground. Members of the underground sneaked aboard the ferry and planted explosive charges below deck. Forty-five minutes into the voyage, the charges exploded. Twenty-six passengers and crew members drowned, and the drums of heavy water rolled overboard and sank to the bottom of the sea.

That action effectively ended Germany's participation in the race for the atomic bomb, but the Allies did not want to take any chances. Groves continued to push for bombing raids on laboratories where it was believed German scientists might be at work on an atomic bomb. An aggressive campaign was organized to identify, locate, and capture or kill scientists who were developing a bomb for Hitler. At the top of this hit list was Werner Heisenberg, the German physicist who had been a highly respected member of the international scientific community before the war.

Although Heisenberg's heavy-water approach to the development of the atomic bomb would never have been successful, Allied scientists did not realize this at the time. All they knew was that the Germans had an active research program in progress and it had to be stopped. Many schemes were devised involving the abduction or assassination of leading German scientists such as Heisenberg, but none was ever carried out.

The closest any of the operations came to fruition was one involving Morris "Moe" Berg, a former catcher for the Boston Red Sox who had retired from professional baseball in January 1942. Berg was an accomplished lawyer and a true intellectual. He was proficient in many languages—French, German, Italian, Japanese, Portuguese, and Spanish among them. He also dabbled at various times in Arabic, Bulgarian, Hebrew, Latin, Mandarin Chinese, Polish, Russian, and Yiddish. Berg first went to work for the U.S. government with the Office of Inter-American Affairs, whose mission was to help the war effort by encouraging friendly relations between the United States and her neighbors in Central and South America.

In 1942 President Roosevelt had authorized the creation of the Office of Special Services (OSS), an espionage unit that became the Central Intelligence Agency (CIA) after the war. The OSS engaged in cloak-and-dagger operations that would greatly aid the war effort. Berg's education, intelligence, proficiency with languages, resourcefulness, and world travel experiences made him an ideal candidate and he was recruited by the OSS. Fellow agent Michael Burke recalled after the war:

> Moe was absolutely ideal for undercover work. . . . One, because of his physical attributes. He could go anyplace without fear. He had stamina . . . he had an alert, quick mind that could adapt itself into any new or strange subject and make him comfortable quickly. He was immensely involved intellectually and active in international affairs through reading and travel. He had the capacity to be at home in Italy or France or London or Bucharest.

Berg was sworn into the OSS in the summer of 1943. A few months later, General Groves recruited him to work on intelligence gathering for the Manhattan Project. Berg's job was to find out how much progress the Germans were making on their atomic weapons program. Berg immersed himself in a crash program of study about nuclear physics. He pored over technical texts in libraries and interviewed American scientists. Berg's investigations led him to the conclusion that Germany had no nuclear weapon and had no hope of acquiring one in the near future. Groves was not convinced. He still considered Heisenberg a major threat.

At one point, there was a plan for Berg to kidnap Heisenberg, but it was abandoned because the risk of Berg being captured by the Nazis was too great. In December 1944 Heisenberg went to Zurich, Switzerland, a neutral country during World War II, to deliver a physics lecture. In the audience was Berg, armed with a pistol and the authority to kill Heisenberg if he thought it necessary. If Heisenberg said anything to convince Berg that the Germans were close to building an atomic bomb, he would

Moe Berg (National Archives)

shoot him on the spot. It would be a suicide mission because there was no way for Berg to escape. Heisenberg spoke on an obscure theory that Berg did not understand at all, but he knew it had nothing to do with developing an atomic bomb.

After the lecture, Berg met with one of his most trusted contacts, Paul Scherrer, director of the Swiss scientific institute that had hosted Heisenberg's lecture. Scherrer told Berg that not only was Heisenberg not working on an atomic bomb, he was also anti-Nazi. Heisenberg himself later confirmed that at a party Berg attended at Scherrer's home. Berg followed Heisenberg out of the party that evening. It would have been the perfect opportunity for him to assassinate Heisenberg, but he was convinced that Heisenberg posed no threat. The two men never saw each other again.

As fearful as Groves and the Manhattan Project scientists were of a program to develop a German bomb, the United States did surprisingly little to find out about it until the war was nearly won. Groves organized an intelligence unit called Alsos. Under the command of Lieutenant Colonel Boris T. Pash, Alsos agents followed advancing Allied armies in Europe, trying to gather whatever information they could. Despite the findings of Berg and other OSS agents, there was lingering fear that if Germany, on the brink of total collapse, did possess any kind of viable nuclear weapons, Hitler would use them in desperation. The first Alsos mission was organized in Italy in December 1943 to obtain information regarding scientific developments. Although some discoveries were made that were of significant use to the Allies, the mission was unable to find any conclusive information about Germany's atomic bomb research. The second Alsos mission was organized in France in August 1944 to follow advancing Allied armies and capture any nuclear-research-related materials along the way.

The third and final Alsos mission, the most successful of the three, entered Germany on February 24, 1945. There was an additional urgency to this mission. None of Germany's nuclear materials or scientists could be allowed to fall into the hands of the Soviets, who were rapidly advancing into Germany from the east. Although the Soviet Union was allied with the United States and other European powers to defeat Germany, there was a great deal of mistrust among the powers. It was widely believed that, with the defeat of Hitler and Nazi Germany, Stalin and the Soviet Union would quickly change from ally to adversary. A key facility, the Auergesellschaft Works just north of Berlin, was identified within what became the Russian zone of occupation. There was no way the Americans could reach it before the Russians, so Groves requested General George C. Marshall, army chief of staff, to order it destroyed. On March 15, 612 B-17s from the Eighth Air Force dropped 2,000 tons of high explosives, totally destroying the plant before the Russians could seize it. In addition, Alsos captured a salt mine in Lansdale that housed an inventory of 1,100 tons of uranium ore.

The mission discovered that Germany had a primitive nuclear weapons program that was years behind the Manhattan Project. There was no possibility of Germany launching a last-ditch nuclear attack. In the final years of the war, Germany concentrated its research and resources on building V-1 and V-2 rockets instead of the atomic bomb. No one knows for sure why the German nuclear program failed. There is continuing debate among historians about whether or not Heisenberg sabotaged the program. Whatever the reason, it was a stroke of good fortune for the Allies that German research took a wrong turn at a critical moment and never recovered.

Great Britain and the United States had good reason to distrust their Russian ally. Soviet spies had been collecting intelligence on the Manhattan Project since its inception. Physicist Klaus Fuchs was the most effective Soviet spy at Los Alamos. Born in Germany, Fuchs became a member of the German Communist Party as a young man. When the Nazis came to power in Germany and began persecuting Communists, Fuchs fled to Great Britain to avoid imprisonment and became a naturalized British citizen. He went to work for the Manhattan Project in 1943. He first worked at Columbia University on uranium separation and later joined the team at Los Alamos. Colleagues regarded Fuchs as a first-rate scientist and researcher, a serious man totally focused on his work. What they did not suspect was that Fuchs was transferring detailed reports of the bomb project to a Soviet courier named Raymond. Fuchs did not have access to all the information at Los Alamos,

Klaus Fuchs, the German-born British atomic scientist who worked on the Manhattan Project at Los Alamos, was convicted in 1950 of passing nuclear secrets to the Soviet Union. Although Fuchs received a more lenient sentence than the Rosenbergs, the information he gave to the Soviets was of far greater value. (Library of Congress)

but he did have access to a great deal of it, and he regularly passed it on to his Soviet contact. Fuchs's contribution to the Soviet atomic bomb program was enormous. The Soviets were able to build and test an atomic bomb of their own in 1949, thanks in large part to the information Fuchs had passed on to them. By that time, the Soviet Union had replaced Germany and Japan as the enemy of the United States and western Europe. The Soviet Union's development of an atomic bomb kicked off a cold war and nuclear arms race that lasted until the Soviet Union collapsed in the late 1980s.

Fuchs was identified as a spy in late 1949. He was arrested in Great Britain for espionage in February 1950. Fuchs's arrest could not have come at a worse time. Two weeks earlier, a jury had convicted a former U.S. State Department official, Alger Hiss, of perjury for denying under oath that he had passed secret information to a Communist agent named Whittaker Chambers. One week following Fuchs's arrest, Senator Joseph McCarthy from Wisconsin was catapulted into the limelight with his erroneous allegation that there were two hundred Communist agents employed by the State Department. Politicians like McCarthy would capitalize on America's fear of the Soviet Union to help manifest an atmosphere of intense paranoia. There was no worse time to be a suspected Communist, especially a suspected Communist spy. Fuchs confessed and identified his contact, "Raymond," as Harry Gold, the son of poor Russian Jewish immigrants whose interest in socialism led him to make contacts with the Communist movement and later Soviet intelligence for espionage work.

Gold implicated additional conspirators, David and Ruth Greenglass. The Greenglasses had joined the Young Communist League in

1943, shortly before David was drafted into the army and eventually assigned to Los Alamos as a machinist. On June 15, 1950, the FBI questioned Greenglass, and he admitted he had passed information on to Gold. He also identified his wife, Ruth, and his brother-in-law, Julius Rosenberg, as participants in the Soviet spy ring. Greenglass told the FBI that through his wife, Rosenberg recruited him to provide notes and sketches relating to a high-explosive lens mold being developed at the Los Alamos laboratories. On July 17, 1950, FBI agents arrested Julius Rosenberg and his wife, Ethel. The couple became the focus of one of the most famous and controversial spy trials in American history.

The FBI's primary interest in arresting Ethel was to use the threat of prosecuting her as a means of getting Julius to talk. The case against Ethel was very weak, resting entirely upon the testimony of the Greenglasses, who said she was present when conversations about the espionage took place. Even with the threat of his wife's prosecution, Julius refused to cooperate. The government prosecuted Ethel as a coconspirator.

Joel Barr, a college friend of Julius Rosenberg, disappeared in Paris upon learning of his arrest. Another college friend, Morton Sobell, boarded a plane with his family at La Guardia Airport in New York City with tickets for Mexico City. Alfred Sarant, another friend of Rosenberg, eluded FBI surveillance and managed to cross the border into Mexico and disappear. When William Perl, a Cleveland scientist, was called to testify before the grand jury about Rosenberg, he denied ever knowing him. Perl was indicted for perjury. A fifth Rosenberg acquaintance, Max Elitcher, cooperated with the FBI, telling investigators that Rosenberg tried to recruit him for espionage work in 1944. The most damning witness against the Rosenbergs was David Greenglass. He provided incriminating details about their espionage activities—burning notes in a frying pan, meeting in cars on dark streets at late hours, and using a Jell-O box for a recognition signal. Ruth Greenglass corroborated her husband's testimony and also incriminated Ethel Rosenberg, alleging that she spent at least one evening typing David's handwritten notes on Los Alamos. Harry Gold was an effective witness for the prosecution, definitively connecting Rosenberg with the Soviet Union's chief of spy operations.

Both Rosenbergs pleaded the Fifth Amendment (the right of an accused person not to testify to avoid self-incrimination) in response to all questions about their membership in the Communist Party. Julius Rosenberg denied all the allegations made by Elitcher, Greenglass, and the other witnesses. It took the eleven-man, one-woman jury only a few hours to deliberate. They found Julius and Ethel Rosenberg guilty of espionage. Judge Irving Kaufman sentenced them to death by the

Julius Rosenberg, in handcuffs, and his wife, Ethel, holding his arm. Accused of spying for the Soviet Union, they were convicted of conspiracy to commit espionage and executed. (Library of Congress)

electric chair. The other conspirators fared better in their trials, receiving prison sentences ranging from five to thirty years.

Letters poured into the White House begging for clemency. The Pope asked for mercy. The Rosenbergs' two young sons, Michael and Robert, marched carrying signs that read "Don't Kill My Mommy and Daddy." After two years of appeals, the Supreme Court upheld the verdict by a vote of five to four. The Rosenbergs were executed at New York's Sing Sing prison in Ossining on the morning of June 19, 1953. Ethel Rosenberg was the first woman executed by the U.S. government since Mary Surratt was hanged for her role in Abraham Lincoln's assassination. Debate continued about the trial for decades, but any lingering doubt about Julius Rosenberg's guilt faded when information released by the National Security Agency in 1995 confirmed he had indeed been a spy. There was, however, no evidence that Ethel Rosenberg had engaged in any espionage work at all.

Six
Trinity

If the radiance of a thousand suns
Were to burst at once into the sky,
That would be like the splendor
of the Mighty One . . .
I am become death,
The Destroyer of worlds.
—The Bhagavad Gita

Work on the Manhattan Project proceeded at a frenetic pace. Two types of weapons were being developed at Los Alamos. The first, a uranium bomb, was long and thin. Originally called "Thin Man," in honor of President Roosevelt, the size of the bomb was cut down and the nickname was changed to "Little Boy." This bomb utilized a type of uranium called U-235. It would be detonated using a modified artillery gun inside a bomb casing to fire a lump of uranium onto a spherical uranium target at two thousand feet per second. The impact of one critical mass onto the other would theoretically create a nuclear explosion. In early 1944 the scientists at Los Alamos faced a crisis. They could not get the quantities of fissionable material they needed. Despite the massive efforts underway, Oak Ridge produced only tiny amounts of pure U-235 through a painfully slow and complicated process. By mid-1945 there would be enough uranium for only one bomb.

The second type of bomb being developed at Los Alamos was a plutonium bomb. Rounder than "Little Boy," it was named "Fat Man" in honor of Winston Churchill, prime minister of Great Britain. Hanford was producing the second type of fissionable material, Pu-239, needed for "Fat Man," and by 1945 it was estimated that there would be enough plutonium for more than one bomb.

The scientists concluded that the relatively simple "gun assembly" method used for the U-235 bomb would not work for plutonium. Two subcritical masses of plutonium could not be brought together fast enough to prevent a premature detonation. Physicist Seth Neddermeyer, a former student of Oppenheimer, proposed surrounding the plutonium with a layer of explosives. The blast wave of the detonated explosives

Workers at an atomic furnace, where radioactive isotopes are "cooked"
(U.S. Department of Energy)

Reactor at Hanford (Atomic Archive)

John von Neumann (MPHPA)

would compress the plutonium instantly into a supercritical mass. This theory of implosion involved an extremely complicated procedure, and most scientists, including Oppenheimer, did not believe it would work.

Neddermeyer's theory became more credible when mathematician John von Neumann calculated that the implosion was feasible and that it would actually require less of the scarce fissionable material than was needed for the gun method. The founder of game theory and a pioneer in computers, von Neumann was considered to be a genius, and the scientific community respected his opinion. The theory of implosion ultimately led to the single most significant breakthrough at Los Alamos. The implosion theory was so secret that the very word remained classified until 1951, six years after the end of World War II.

Neddermeyer's implosion method had to be tested before it could be implemented, but that meant testing the most potentially destructive weapon ever known somewhere in America.

Oppenheimer, who referred to the plutonium bomb as "the Gadget," began searching for a suitable testing site in May 1944. The area had to be relatively flat so that the effects of the blast on the terrain would be minimal. The weather had to be relatively good and reliable. The site had to be isolated from any centers of population, but also close enough to Los Alamos to allow for the easy movement of men and equipment, as a great deal of experimentation and observation was necessary.

An area appropriately called Jornada del Muerto was chosen as the test site. Translated from the Spanish, the name means "Journey of Death." Lying between present-day Socorro, New Mexico, and El Paso, Texas, Jornada del Muerto is a stretch of high desert bounded by the San Andreas and San Mateos mountains. In the early 1940s the region had only a few isolated cattle and sheep ranches. When the war began, the federal government leased several hundred square miles to be used for test bombing. This area became known as the Alamogordo Bombing Range.

Jumbo, the proposed container for the implosion bomb that was never used (MPHPA)

Interior of building S-24 at Los Alamos (MPHPA)

The scientists were so uncertain about whether or not "the Gadget" would work that they proposed putting it inside an enormous steel container. If the bomb worked, the container would be instantly vaporized. If it did not work, the scientists speculated that the blast would be contained and the precious plutonium could be recovered. When it was finally constructed, the container, called Jumbo, weighed 214 tons and had 15-inch-thick walls of banded steel. Jumbo arrived at the test site in April 1945, the heaviest single object ever moved by railroad. By that time, however, it was decided the enormous contraption was not needed after all. There was increased confidence in Neddermeyer's implosion theory. Groves would later unsuccessfully try to blow up Jumbo using conventional explosives because he did not want congressional investigators to ask why so much money had been spent on something that was never used.

The test site was designated Trinity, but no one is certain why. Although he never confirmed this, Oppenheimer most likely named the site. It may refer to a devotional poem by English poet John Donne that Oppenheimer had mentioned to colleagues. The poem opens with the verse: "Batter my heart, three person'd God." The name may also reflect Oppenheimer's great interest in the Hindu religion. In the Hindu concept of Trinity, there is Brahma, the Creator; Vishnu, the Preserver; and Shiva, the Destroyer. Hindus believe that whatever exists in the universe cannot be destroyed. It can only be transformed. When one part dies in the cycle of life, another is created from it.

On March 15, 1945, President Roosevelt was told that an atomic bomb would be ready for testing by summer. In April, Oak Ridge finally produced enough uranium for a single bomb. The material was shipped to Los Alamos, where physicists assembled "Little Boy" by hand. At about the same time, the scientists working on "the Gadget" announced that they had a device ready for testing.

Then on April 12 President Roosevelt died of a cerebral hemorrhage while on vacation. Roosevelt had served the nation as president for twelve years, longer than any other before or since. He had pulled the country out of the Great Depression, the worst economic crisis in U.S. history, and he led the country to incredible victories during World War II. The sixty-three-year-old president's health had been failing for months, but this was known only by those closest to him. When Roosevelt died, the nation was stunned.

On April 12, 1945, at 7:09 P.M., Vice President Harry S Truman took the oath of office in a ceremony that lasted a minute. He had only been vice president since January 20. An hour later he was told about the atomic bomb. Truman was barely known by the American public. He had had an undistinguished career as a senator from Missouri, and as vice president was regarded as only a figurehead. He was not close to

EXTRA **The Knoxville Journal** EXTRA

Tennessee Valley's Greatest Newspaper

KNOXVILLE, TENNESSEE, THURSDAY, APRIL 12, 1945

FDR IS DEAD

Ninth Army Sweeps Across Elbe To Wide Open Road To Berlin

of Nuernberg

The Seventh Army captured Schweinfurt, a ballbearing manufacturing center of 42,000 population, while farther to the southwest the French First Army took the Black Forest cities of Baden-Baden and Rastatt.

On the northern end of the front, the British Second Army captured Celle, a German training center for gas warfare 50 miles south of Hamburg, and deepened its Aller River bridgehead thrust within 45 miles of that second greatest German city.

Shift Of AAF Set 30 Days After V-E

WASHINGTON, April 12 (AP)—General movements of Army Air Forces from Europe to the Pacific will wait until at least 30 days after V-E day. Some "critical" units may be shifted earlier.

An air force spokesman disclosing this yesterday and it would take a month or more to put into effect the administration for such a vast transfer. Some units will be assigned to a "relatively small" occupational air force in Europe.

Emphasizing that the air forces intend to do to Japan what they have already done to Germany, the spokesman said all the air strength that can be employed will be thrown against the Nips. The only limiting factor will be land available for bases.

Many To Come Home

Some units will be sent by the way of the United States, with numerous men given home leave. Many will be redeployed by other routes.

During the early phases of deployment, the spokesman said, there will be no substantial demobilization of AAF personnel except for those eligible men already in the United States.

None will be demobilized until their adjusted rating scores have been published throughout the Army. Their release may be still further delayed by the lack of a qualified replacement, if they are "essential" men, or by some necessity which is unforeseen now.

The AAF is using the Army scoring procedure to determine eligibility for demobilization and expects to release the same percentage as the other Army branches.

Personnel readjustments of all units to be redeployed will be made before the units are dispatched.

Sarge On Leave Nabs Two Escaped Germans In Utah

Loss Of 500 Queen Bees Told By Georgia Shipper

VALDOSTA, Ga., April 12 (AP)—Five hundred queen bees were missing today from the hives of G. G. Puett of nearby Hahira, one of the nation's leading bee shippers.

Wynn Buys Briscoe Building For $60,000

PRESIDENT FRANKLIN DELANO ROOSEVELT

President Dies Suddenly At Warm Springs

Cerebral Hemorrhage Fatal To Roosevelt

By D. HAROLD OLIVER

WARM SPRINGS, Ga., April 12 (AP)—President Franklin D. Roosevelt died unexpectedly today of a cerebral hemorrhage, at 3:35 p. m. (Central War Time) at his summer cottage here.

The White House announced late today that President Roosevelt had died of cerebal hemorrhage.

> WASHINGTON, April 12 (AP)—Chairman Connally (D. Tex.) of the Senate Foreign Relations Committee said tonight the United Nations Conference in San Francisco may have to be postponed because of President Roosevelt's death.

The death occurred this afternoon at Warm Springs, Ga. A White House statement said:

"Vice President Truman has been notified. He was called to the White House and informed by Mrs. Roosevelt. The secretary of state has been advised. A cabinet meeting has been called.

"The four Roosevelt boys in the service have been sent a message by their mother, which said the President slept away this afternoon. He did his job to the end, as he would want to do.

Bless you all, and all our love, added Mrs. Roosevelt. She signed the message mother.

Funeral services will be held Saturday afternoon in the east room of the White House. Interment will be at Hyde Park Sunday afternoon. No detailed arrangements or times have been decided upon as yet.

Harry S. Truman, former senator, Missouri county judge and one-time Kansas City haberdasher, by Mr. Roosevelt's death moves up to the highest office in the land.

At the Capitol, aides of Truman disclosed he had left the White House only a few minutes before the news was made public.

Mr. Roosevelt had been at Warm Springs for more than a week. Stephen Early, presidential secretary, informed reporters:

"Mrs. Roosevelt, Adm. Ross McIntyre (the Roosevelt physician) and I will leave Washington by air this afternoon for Warm Springs."

Vice President Truman was at work in his office when the news came. He received a call about 5:25 p. m. A few minutes later secret servicemen came and whisked him away to the White House in an automobile.

Matt Connelly, Truman's executive assistant, said he assumed that the new President would take the oath at once but that he did not know any details.

Truman's vice presidential staff stood around his office in the senate office building, their faces pale as though they had been stunned by the unexpected news which lifted the former Missouri farm boy into the highest office in the nation's giving.

The death of the President was announced a few short minutes after it was revealed that high Army officials had told senators the war soon would be over in Germany.

Cabinet members began assembling at 6 p. m.

Yanks Retake Vital Ridge On Okinawa

Russian Armored Forces Cut Last Lifelines North Of Vienna

Bulletins

SHIPS RAID SABANG

LONDON, April 12 (Thursday), INS—The Jap Domei Agency reported today that an Allied task force, including British battleships of the Queen Elizabeth type, raided Sabang, Jap-held base in the northwestern tip of Sumatra.

PRIETO IN WASHINGTON

WASHINGTON, April 11 (AP)—Indalecio Prieto, former war minister of Republican Spain, has arrived in Washington from Mexico as a guest of the American Federation of Labor to discuss international labor problems.

BREAK WITH SPAIN SOUGHT

'Early Christmas Tot' Can Quit His Hospital Cot Soon

The front page of The Knoxville Journal, *Thursday, April 12, 1945. President Roosevelt's death came as a great shock. (U.S. Department of Energy)*

A billboard reminding Manhattan Project workers that there is still one enemy left to defeat (U.S. Department of Energy)

Roosevelt and never expected to succeed him as president. Truman knew there was a large secret war project underway, but he had no clear idea about what it was. It would be over a week after Truman was sworn in as president of the United States before General Groves was called in to provide a complete briefing on the Manhattan Project.

Events then moved rapidly. On May 8, 1945, the unconditional surrender of Germany was announced. The war in Europe was over. The Manhattan Project had been started to defeat Hitler and Nazi Germany, but now Hitler had committed suicide and Germany was beaten. The war in Asia, however, was far from over. Japan was clearly going to be defeated, but the Japanese proved to be tenacious and unwilling to surrender, even in the face of overwhelming odds. There were also the Soviets to consider. The remarkably resilient Soviet Union had rebounded from invasion and near defeat by Germany. Stalin was making aggressive moves in Eastern Europe. It was becoming increasingly clear that Stalin and the Soviet Union would become a new enemy of Great Britain and the United States. On July 16, 1945, the "Big Three"—Churchill, Stalin, and Truman—met in Potsdam, Germany, to discuss the future of Europe and the course of the war in Asia. If Truman, a new president with no international negotiating experience, could have news of a successful atomic bomb test, he would be able to negotiate with Stalin from a position of great strength.

General Groves set July 16 as the date for the Trinity test, but mid-July was not an ideal time. Temperatures in that part of the desert often rose to well over one hundred degrees Fahrenheit and severe thunderstorms were common. In addition to potentially problematic weather, a sufficient quantity of plutonium did not arrive from Hanford until May

General Groves sets his sights upon Japan. (U.S. Department of Energy)

31. Nobody at Los Alamos had ever handled or even seen plutonium before. The bomb had been pure theory up to that point—notes and calculations on blackboards. The plutonium arrived in the form of a syrupy nitrate that had to be purified and solidified through a complicated process.

Many problems arose at the last minute, but there was not as much time to fix them as the scientists would have liked. Time was of the essence, and improvisation was necessary. At one point, scientists had to grind the plutonium spheres using dental drills. No one knew how such improvisations would work. The plutonium core arrived at the Trinity site on July 12. It rode in the backseat of an army sedan in a case studded with rubber bumpers. Prior to its arrival, an old ranch house at the site had been meticulously vacuumed and its windows sealed to keep out the dust. There, preliminary assembly of the bomb was done on a kitchen table.

On July 13, the plutonium core was taken to the base of a one-hundred-foot-tall tower at the Trinity site for final assembly. Panic

The plutonium core is loaded into a car for delivery to the Trinity test site. (Atomic Archive)

Herb Lehr, a member of the Manhattan Project's Special Engineer Detachment (SED), delivers the plutonium core for "the Gadget." (Atomic Archive)

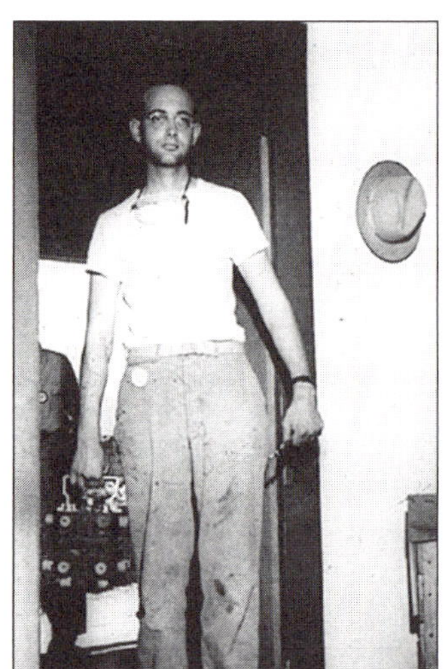

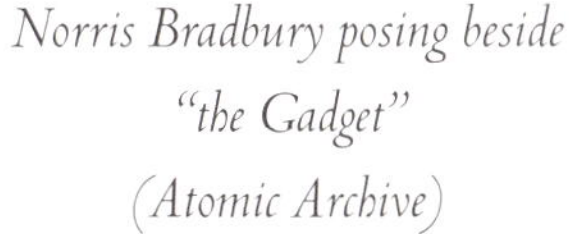

Norris Bradbury posing beside "the Gadget" (Atomic Archive)

Scientists raising "the Gadget" to the top of the tower (Atomic Archive)

ensued when the core would not click into place. The operation had been rehearsed a hundred times, but something unanticipated had gone wrong. The intense desert heat had expanded the plutonium core. Within a few minutes, the temperature of the bomb assembly had cooled the core down, and it finally clicked into position.

"The Gadget" perched atop the tower at Trinity (Atomic Archive)

Several buses and carloads of observers arrived at the site on the night of July 15. They would watch the test at what was assumed to be a safe distance—20 miles northwest of ground zero. There were observation posts much closer. Sheltered bunkers with concrete roofs were located only 5.7 miles from ground zero. Several of them were equipped with special photographic and scientific equipment. All airports within 100 miles of the test site were ordered to ban aircraft from the area. General Groves, always obsessed with security, was concerned about saboteurs infiltrating the test site. Soldiers armed with submachine guns patrolled ground zero. Explosives expert George Kistiakowsky and his team were ordered to guard the tower before the test. An angry Kistiakowsky, thinking Groves's extreme security precautions were unnecessary, had to spend the night perched atop the tower.

The scientists wagered bets of one dollar each on the size of the bomb's blast. The most pessimistic scientist bet "the Gadget" would be a complete dud. Edward Teller placed the most optimistic bet, wagering the blast would equal forty-five thousand tons of TNT. Oppenheimer's bet of three hundred tons was considered the most realistic. Physicist Isidor I. Rabi, arriving a few days after the pool began, was left with eighteen thousand tons for his bet.

The test was scheduled for 4:00 A.M., but thunderstorms moved in. Lightning hit ground zero at one point and knocked out one of the searchlights illuminating the tower. There was the erroneous fear that lightning might actually set off the bomb. Trying to outguess the weather, Groves and Oppenheimer rescheduled the test for 5:30 A.M., weather permitting.

At approximately 5:00 A.M., the arming party headed by Kistiakowsky checked the electrical connections at the tower, threw the final switches, and then raced their jeeps to the control bunker five miles away to join Oppenheimer. Groves joined the observers 20 miles northwest of ground zero. Not knowing what would happen upon detonation, the soldiers were ordered to wear combat helmets for the test. The scientists also took meaningless precautions. Teller wore heavy gloves and a pair of extra dark sunglasses under his welder's goggles, and he smeared his face with sunscreen for protection against ultraviolet rays.

The tension among the observers was intense. No one knew for sure what would happen when the bomb was detonated. Edwin McMillan, one of the discoverers of plutonium, said this to his wife before he left for the Trinity site:

> We ourselves are not absolutely certain what will happen. In spite of calculations, we are going into the unknown. We know that there are three possibilities. One, that we all [may] be blown to bits if it is more powerful than we expect. Two, it may be a complete dud. Three, it may, as we hope, be a success, we pray without loss of any lives.

Rabi remembers: "We were lying there, very tense, in the early dawn, and there were just a few streaks of gold in the east; you could see your neighbor very dimly." Sam Allison, a University of Chicago physicist, began the countdown at zero minus twenty minutes. A rocket that was to be fired as a two-minute warning fizzled out, but the one-minute warning rocket and siren went off as planned. At 5:29:45 A.M. mountain standard time, Allison yelled "zero." There was nothing at first, and then the sky was ignited by a flash as bright as the sun. The flash was seen in three states. A popular story that surfaced years later told of an eighteen-year-old blind girl named Georgia Green who saw light when she was traveling in a car with her brother-in-law fifty miles from the Trinity site.

The sound was deafening. Windows 125 miles away shattered. Oppenheimer's brother Frank recorded what he heard: "And the thunder from the blast. It bounced on the rocks, and then it went—I don't know where else it bounced. But it never seemed to stop. Not like an ordinary echo with thunder. It just kept echoing back and forth . . . it was a very scary time when it went off."

The blast threw out a multicolored mushroom cloud that surged thirty-eight thousand feet up into the atmosphere over approximately seven minutes. The immediate blast area was engulfed in thick smoke for over an hour. The heat at the center of the blast approximated that of the center of the sun, and the flash of light the blast produced was brighter than twenty suns. The light could be clearly seen in Albuquerque and Santa Fe, New Mexico; Silver City, Nevada; El Paso, Texas; and other points as far as 180 miles away. The blast left a crater a half mile across. The intense heat fused the sand into a greenish gray glass. Every living thing within a mile of ground zero was vaporized. The spectacle reminded Oppenheimer of a line from The Bhagavad Gita, a sacred Hindu text: "I am become Death, the destroyer of worlds!" Rabi recorded what he saw that morning:

> Suddenly there was an enormous flash of light, the brightest light I have ever seen or that I think anyone has ever seen. It blasted; it pounced; it bored its way right through you. It was a vision which was seen with more than the eye. It was seen to last forever. You wish it would stop; altogether it lasted about two seconds. Finally, it was over, diminishing, and we looked toward the place where the bomb had been; there was an enormous ball of fire which grew and grew and it rolled as it grew; it went up into the air, in yellow flashes and into scarlet and green. It looked menacing.

The explosion of "the Gadget" at the Trinity test site in Alamogordo, New Mexico, July 16, 1945 (National Archives)

At ground zero only a few twisted pieces of the steel tower from which the bomb had hung remained still visible in the cement foundation. Measurements taken after the blast indicated the bomb's yield was 18,600 tons. Rabi won the $102 pot in the betting pool.

Only a few of the scores of expensive instruments placed in the blast area to measure the bomb's impact survived. The electromagnetic storm completely paralyzed sensitive gauges and measurement recorders. Radioactive gases penetrated equipment, ruining them with condensation. The bomb's blinding light rendered the cameras virtually useless. Those not protected by thick shields of lead were completely destroyed; even those surrounded by sand and concrete barriers had their film ruined by the tremendous gamma-ray emissions. Most of the film that was salvaged had been fogged by the intense radiation.

It would be weeks before the total impact of the Trinity bomb could be assessed, but it was apparent to everyone by midmorning of July 16 that the bomb had surpassed all expectations and predictions. The test confirmed that Neddermeyer's implosion theory was correct and that it was probably the most efficient way to detonate an atomic weapon.

"The Gadget" also emitted a tremendous amount of radiation. The radioactivity created a reverse smothering effect that weakened the blast power of the bomb at great distances. If the bomb had been detonated from a high level, the radioactivity would have been considerably less and the blast power significantly greater. The Trinity test confirmed the scientists' judgment that "Little Boy" should be detonated from a high altitude.

General Groves and Dr. Oppenheimer examine the remains of the tower from which "the Gadget" was detonated. (Library of Congress)

Those who witnessed the blast experienced a range of emotions, from awe to horror to relief to joy. Kistiakowsky rushed up to Oppenheimer and hugged him. Test director Kenneth Bainbridge said to Oppenheimer, "Now we're all sons of bitches." The initial response was elation—the blast was greeted with applause, cheers, and triumphant howls of celebration. A memorandum to the secretary of war, Brigadier General Thomas F. Farrell, who witnessed the explosion from the forward bunker ten thousand yards from ground zero, offered this vivid appraisal:

> The effects could well be called unprecedented, magnificent, beautiful, stupendous and terrifying. No man-made phenomenon of such tremen-

> dous power had ever occurred before. The lighting effects beggared description. The whole country was lighted by a searing light with the intensity many times that of the midday sun. It was golden, purple, violet, gray and blue. It lighted every peak, crevasse and ridge of the nearby mountain range with a clarity and beauty that cannot be described but must be seen to be imagined. It was that beauty the great poets dream about but describe most poorly and inadequately. Thirty seconds after the explosion came, first, the air blast pressing hard against the people and things, to be followed almost immediately by the strong, sustained awesome roar which warned of doomsday and made us feel that we puny things were blasphemous to dare tamper with the forces heretofore reserved to The Almighty.

Several eyewitness accounts of the test use religious imagery like Farrell's. Physicist Victor Weisskopf said the explosion reminded him "of the medieval picture of Christ's ascension." One of the most lyrical descriptions came from William L. Laurence:

> The Atomic Age began at exactly 5:30 Mountain War Time on the morning of July 16, 1945, on a stretch of semi-desert land about 50 airline miles from Alamogordo, N.M., just a few minutes before the dawn of a new day on that part of the earth.
>
> Just at that instant there rose from the bowels of the earth a light not of the world, the light of many suns in one. It was sunrise such as the world has never seen, a great green super-sun climbing in a fraction of a second to a height of more than 8,000 feet, rising even higher until it touched the clouds, lighting up earth and sky all around with a dazzling luminosity.
>
> Up it went, a great ball of fire about a mile in diameter, changing colors as it kept shooting upward, from deep purple to orange, expanding, growing bigger, rising as it was expanding, an elemental force freed from its bonds after being chained for billions of years.
>
> For a fleeting instant the color was unearthly green, such as one sees

> only in the corona of the sun during a total eclipse. It was as though the earth had opened and the skies had split.
>
> One felt as though he had been privileged to witness the Birth of the World—to be present at the moment of Creation when the Lord said: "Let There Be Light."

Kistiakowsky likened the experience more to apocalypse than creation: "I am sure that at the end of the world—in the last millisecond of the earth's existence—the last men will see what we saw." The historic event prompted many to make philosophical observations such as this one from Rabi:

> At first I was thrilled. It was a vision. Then a few minutes afterward, I had goose flesh all over me when I realized what this meant for the future of humanity. . . . The new powers represented a threat not only to mankind but to all forms of life: the seas and the air. One could foresee that nothing was immune from the tremendous powers of these new forces.

Norris Bradbury had a more practical view of the outcome: "Some people claim to have wondered at the time about the future of mankind. I didn't. We were at war and the damned thing worked." A pleased General Groves succinctly called the test "successful beyond the most optimistic expectations of anyone."

The bomb remained a closely guarded secret for another month after Trinity, but an event of such magnitude could not be kept entirely under wraps. Several hundred civilians had witnessed the explosion. Some people thought it was an earthquake; others were certain a meteor had fallen to earth. Lewis Farris of Carrizozo, New Mexico, ran up the main street of town shouting, "Hell's broken out someplace. It must be Japs." The army immediately released an official statement:

> Several inquiries have been received concerning a heavy explosion which occurred on the Alamogordo Air Base reservation this morning. A remotely controlled ammunition magazine containing a considerable amount of high explosives and pyrotechnics exploded. There was no loss of life or injury to anyone, and the property damage outside of the explosives magazine was negligible.

The War Department pressured local newspapers not to report any background information, details, or speculations about other explanations for the blast. Most of them cooperated. A Chicago newspaper received a call from a man who had been traveling through the area, who spoke in great detail about the crash of a giant meteorite. The reporter who wrote the story was visited by FBI agents the following day and was asked not to write anything more about "the meteorite."

President Truman received word of the successful test while he was in Potsdam. He was in desperate need of good news. He had arrived at Potsdam intending to persuade the Soviet Union to enter the war with Great Britain and the United States against Japan. In light of this news about the bomb, it was no longer an urgent issue. Truman had planned to tell Stalin about the bomb's existence, but he now had a new plan. He would tell the Soviet premier after the formal sessions were over. At the end of the conference, Truman walked around the conference table to Stalin and his interpreter and casually mentioned that the United States "had a new weapon of unusual destructive force."

Stalin showed no particular interest in the news, saying simply that he was glad to hear it and hoped it could be put to good use against the Japanese. Truman and Churchill were delighted with Stalin's lack of interest, believing he did not realize the importance of what he had been told. But Stalin was no fool. His seeming lack of interest in Truman's remark was due to his already knowing about the bomb. Soviet spies had been monitoring the Manhattan Project for some time.

The successful test of "the Gadget" effectively ended the Manhattan Project, although intensive research continued at Los Alamos. The mission of the Manhattan Project—to develop a weapon of mass destruction in order to win the war—had been accomplished. Germany was finished and the defeat of Japan was inevitable, but the road to final victory still looked long and bloody. There was no doubt among those working on the project that the bomb would be used against Japan if it did not surrender immediately and unconditionally. Japan had a small nuclear weapons research program of its own, but it was too primitive to produce a bomb. Should an atomic bomb be used against the Japanese when for all intents and purposes they were defeated? This was a question that troubled many in the days following Trinity.

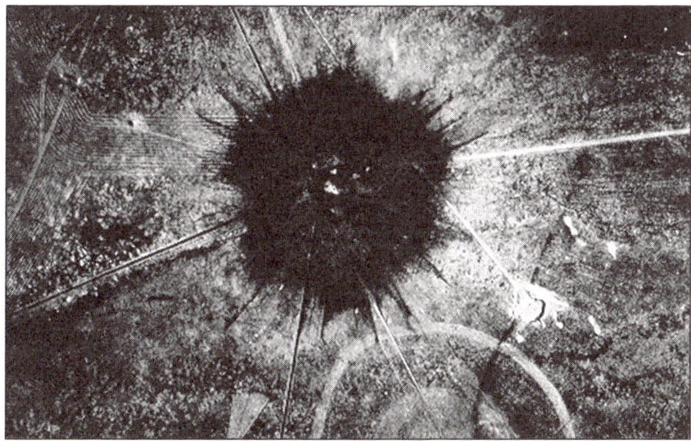

Aerial veiw of ground zero at Trinity
(MPHPA)

Seven
Judgment Day

We are now prepared to obliterate more rapidly and completely every productive enterprise the Japanese have above ground in any city. We shall destroy their docks, their factories, and their communications. Let there be no mistake; we shall completely destroy Japan's power to make war.
—President Harry S Truman

A month before the Trinity test, on June 18, 1945, Secretary of War Henry L. Stimson, Assistant Secretary of War John J. McCloy, and representatives from the branches of the armed forces met with President Truman at the White House for a strategy meeting. General Marshall opened the meeting with a briefing on the plans for invading Japan. Predictions for the outcome of the invasion were grim. General Marshall estimated one hundred thousand American servicemen would be killed in the initial landings, followed by thirty-one thousand casualties in the next thirty days of the campaign. He further estimated that 20 million Japanese civilians would be killed in the course of the campaign.

Marshall's horrific predictions were considered realistic. In the last two major battles with the Japanese, on Iwo Jima and Okinawa, casualty rates were appallingly high for both sides, but especially for the Japanese, who fought to the last man defending both islands. The forty-eight thousand recent American casualties in the battle for Okinawa were fresh in everyone's mind. The Japanese would be even more zealous in the defense of their home islands. In preparation for this invasion,

Secretary of War Henry L. Stimson expressed great apprehensions about dropping the bomb on Japan. He tried to persuade President Truman to consider other alternatives. (Library of Congress)

Japanese teenage boys were training to strap explosives to their bodies and hurl themselves at tanks. Girls were equipped with carpenters' awls to use against American soldiers they believed would try to rape them. An invasion of Japan would mean death and destruction on an unimaginable scale.

Depending on the progress of the invasion, Marshall speculated that the war could drag on into late 1946. Representatives from the air force and navy agreed with Marshall that air and naval power alone would not be enough to make Japan capitulate. President Truman unenthusiastically authorized the planning of Operation Downfall, a massive, two-phase invasion of Japan's home islands that would involve more than a million American military personnel under the command of General Douglas MacArthur. While invasion forces assembled for Operation Downfall, the Trinity test was conducted at Alamogordo.

In the days following the Trinity test, the mood of many Manhattan Project scientists turned solemn. There was great apprehension about using the atomic bomb both before Trinity and after. Witnessing the awesome destructive power they helped create, many scientists paused to consider the moral consequences of their actions. Why were they continuing to work on the bomb when Germany was defeated? That, after all, had been the reason for the existence of the Manhattan Project—to build an atomic weapon before the Nazis did. Was it morally right to use the bomb against Japan, a virtually defeated enemy with no nuclear capability? How would this terrible thing they created change the world?

Before Trinity, Leo Szilard had made dire speculations that proved prophetic. Szilard predicted the Soviet Union would soon become a nuclear power, and dropping the bomb on Japan would start a nuclear arms race between Russia and the United States that could result in the mutual destruction of both countries. Many of Szilard's colleagues concurred. A recently naturalized American citizen, Szilard studied the U.S. Constitution and the First Amendment's guarantee of the right "to petition Government for a redress of grievances." Szilard thought a petition would be a perfect way to bring to President Truman's attention the concerns of the antibomb scientists. With the help of physicists James Franck and Eugene Wigner, Szilard, who as much as anyone was responsible for getting the Manhattan Project started, circulated petitions at Met Lab and Oak Ridge. A petition dated July 17, 1945, the day after Trinity, addressed to President Truman and signed by Szilard and sixty-nine other scientists, read in part:

> We, the undersigned scientists, have been working in the field of atomic power. Until recently, we have had to fear that the United States might be attacked by atomic bombs during this war and that her only defense might lie in a counterattack by the same means. Today, with the defeat of Germany, this danger is averted and we feel impelled to say what follows:

> The war has to be brought speedily to a successful conclusion and attacks by atomic bombs may very well be an effective method of warfare. We feel, however, that such attacks on Japan could not be justified, at least not unless the terms which will be imposed after the war on Japan were made public in detail and Japan were given the opportunity to surrender. . . .
>
> The development of atomic power will provide the nations with new means of destruction. The atomic bombs at our disposal represent only the first step in this direction, and there is almost no limit to the destructive power which will become available in the course of their future development. Thus a nation which sets the precedent of using these newly liberated forces of nature for purposes of destruction may have to bear the responsibility of opening the door to an era of devastation on an unimaginable scale.

Oppenheimer was furious when he learned of the petitions. He admonished Szilard and the other petitioners for using their prestige as a platform to air political pronouncements. Neither the petition from Met Lab nor the one from Oak Ridge reached the desk of President Truman until after the war.

Even military and political leaders had apprehensions about using an atomic bomb against Japan. Secretary of War Stimson was alone among Truman's closest advisers in his concern about the long-term consequences of using an atomic weapon. In his diary he referred to the bomb as "the thing," "the dire," "the dreadful," "the terrible," and "the diabolical." Admiral Chester Nimitz and General Dwight Eisenhower, two of the highest-ranking military commanders, also voiced their disapproval. Stimson urged President Truman to form an advisory committee to gather as much expert advice as he could.

Many alternatives were considered: a "demonstration" at which a test bomb would be dropped on an uninhabited island in the Pacific with invited Japanese scientists present; a full disclosure to Japan of what the United States planned to do if Japan did not surrender; warning Japan of the imminent bombing to allow time for evacuation, and so on. There had even been a suggestion that Japanese scientists be invited to witness the Trinity test.

Assistant Secretary of War McCloy said, "We should have our heads examined if we don't consider a political solution." He proposed to President Truman that he send the Japanese a personal message offering them honorable surrender, including retention of the emperor as a constitutional monarch, but that this gesture be coupled with the ultimatum that rejection of the proposal would bring on the use of the atomic bomb.

Only President Truman's military adviser, Admiral William Leahy, liked McCloy's proposal. Truman told McCloy that any mention of the bomb to the Japanese was out of the question. Groves had convinced Truman that secrecy, stealth, and surprise were advantages that could not be compromised. The decision to drop the bomb without warning had already been made. The momentum was now too great for it not to be used. The hard-won battles at Iwo Jima and Okinawa convinced many American military leaders that the Japanese were determined to fight to the last man for every inch of ground. Most were convinced the only alternative to using the atomic bomb against Japan was an invasion of the home islands, resulting in hundreds of thousands of American casualties and millions of civilian Japanese dead. Truman was not about to commit political suicide by refusing to use a two-billion-dollar bomb that would save thousands of American lives.

Another urgent concern was the Soviet Union. Truman did not want Stalin to declare war on Japan, because concessions would then have to be made to the Soviet Union when the Japanese surrendered and a peace treaty was signed. There were also the wishes of the late President Roosevelt to consider. Although Roosevelt had left no written policy regarding use of the bomb, he was not known to have considered any action other than to use it when it became available. Years after the war, McCloy bitterly remarked that Groves and Truman had opened a "nuclear Pandora's box. They didn't step back to get the whole picture . . . they didn't look ahead."

On July 26, President Truman issued—on behalf of himself, the president of the nationalist government in China, and the prime minis-

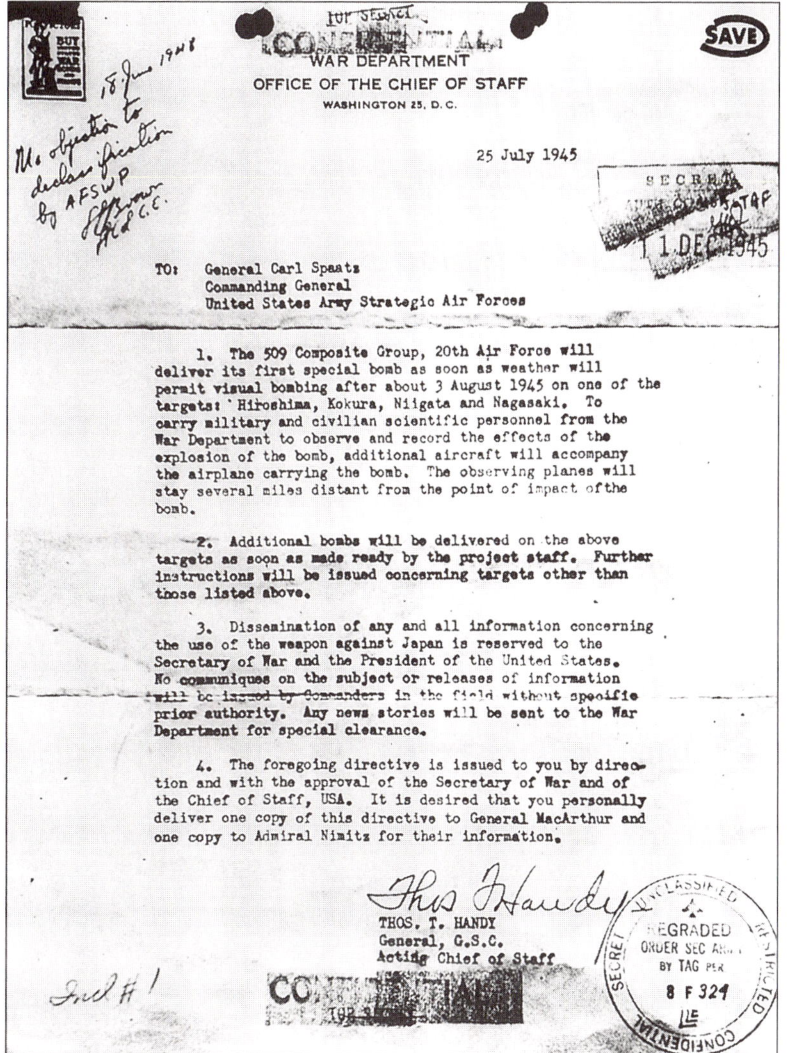

CONFIDENTIAL

WAR DEPARTMENT
OFFICE OF THE CHIEF OF STAFF
WASHINGTON 25, D. C.

18 June 1948
No objection to declassification by AFSWP

25 July 1945

SECRET
11 DEC 1945

TO: General Carl Spaatz
Commanding General
United States Army Strategic Air Forces

1. The 509 Composite Group, 20th Air Force will deliver its first special bomb as soon as weather will permit visual bombing after about 3 August 1945 on one of the targets: Hiroshima, Kokura, Niigata and Nagasaki. To carry military and civilian scientific personnel from the War Department to observe and record the effects of the explosion of the bomb, additional aircraft will accompany the airplane carrying the bomb. The observing planes will stay several miles distant from the point of impact of the bomb.

2. Additional bombs will be delivered on the above targets as soon as made ready by the project staff. Further instructions will be issued concerning targets other than those listed above.

3. Dissemination of any and all information concerning the use of the weapon against Japan is reserved to the Secretary of War and the President of the United States. No communiques on the subject or releases of information will be issued by Commanders in the field without specific prior authority. Any news stories will be sent to the War Department for special clearance.

4. The foregoing directive is issued to you by direction and with the approval of the Secretary of War and of the Chief of Staff, USA. It is desired that you personally deliver one copy of this directive to General MacArthur and one copy to Admiral Nimitz for their information.

Thos T Handy
THOS. T. HANDY
General, G.S.C.
Acting Chief of Staff

Incl #1

CONFIDENTIAL

UNCLASSIFIED
REGRADED
ORDER SEC ARMY
BY TAG PER
8 F 329
SECRET RESTRICTED CONFIDENTIAL

The letter authorizing the dropping of the first atomic bomb (National Archives) ter of Great Britain—the Potsdam Declaration, a document that called for the immediate, unconditional surrender of Japan. The ultimatum read in part: "There are no alternatives. We shall brook no delay. . . . We call upon the government of Japan to proclaim now the unconditional surrender of all Japanese armed forces . . . the alternative for Japan is prompt and utter destruction." The atomic bomb was not specifically mentioned—the Japanese would receive no warning about the bomb if they refused to capitulate.

"Little Boy" specifications (MPHPA)

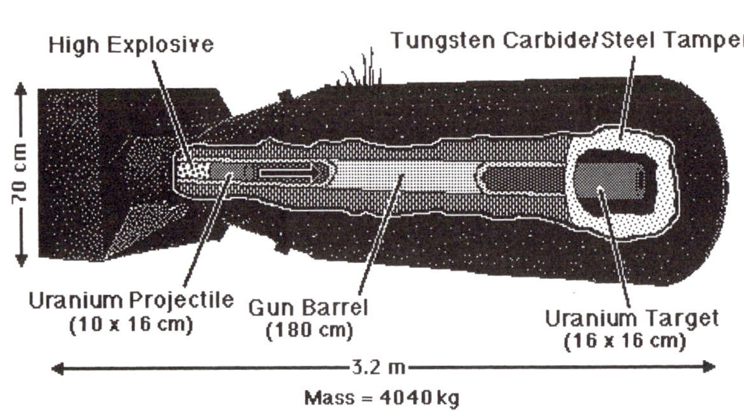

"Little Boy"

Weight: 9,700 lbs

Length: 10 ft.; Diameter: 28 in.

Fuel: Highly enriched uranium-235; "Oralloy" – Produced at Oak Ridge, TN

Uranium Fuel: approx. 140 lbs; target - 85 lbs and projectile - 55 lbs

Target case, barrel, uranium projectile, and other main parts ferried to Tinian Island via USS Indianapolis

Uranium target component ferried to Tinian via C-54 aircraft of the 509th Composite Group

Approx. 1.38% of the uranium fuel (30.9 ounces) actually fissioned

Explosive force: 15,000 tons of TNT equivalent

Use: Dropped on Japanese city of Hiroshima; August 6, 1945

Nuclear Weaponeer: Navy Capt. William Parsons

Delivery: B-29 "Enola Gay" piloted by Col. Paul Tibbets

On the same day that Truman issued the Potsdam Declaration, the heavy cruiser USS *Indianapolis* dropped anchor a thousand yards off Tinian, a tiny island in the Pacific Ocean, and unloaded a fifteen-foot wooden crate containing the firing mechanism for the "Little Boy" bomb. The U-235 core, the explosive fuel for the bomb developed at the Oak Ridge laboratories, was carried in a bucket. The core would be placed inside "Little Boy" and dropped on Hiroshima. Four days later, while en route to the Philippines to join the armada assembling for the invasion of Japan, the *Indianapolis* was torpedoed by the Japanese submarine *I-58.* It sank in twelve minutes. The hasty distress signals sent were either ignored or misinterpreted. Eighty-five hours passed before survivors were spotted by a plane flying overhead and rescued. There was no time to launch lifeboats before the ship sank, so the majority of the survivors, who gathered together in clusters, were kept afloat by life jackets. Of the 1,196-man crew, only 315 were rescued. Twice that many men had survived the sinking, but in the three and a half days in the water, hundreds had been devoured by sharks. Others not eaten by sharks succumbed to dehydration, exhaustion, hypothermia, madness, or wounds suffered in the torpedo attack. This disaster further inflamed Americans against the Japanese.

As expected, the Japanese rejected the Potsdam Declaration, and the plan to use the atomic bomb went forward. In the years following the war, there was much speculation about President Truman's struggle with the decision to drop the bomb, but the reality is that his decision had been firmly made in the summer of 1945; he never questioned whether or not the bomb should be used. Winston Churchill later recalled that use of the bomb "was never an issue." Many of the Los Alamos scientists had strong reservations about using the bombs, but without Oppenheimer on their side, their power of persuasion was weak. General Groves was all for their use against Japan. The military and political leaders who believed the bombing unnecessary were in the minority. By the summer of 1945, momentum for using the bomb against Japan was so strong that all objections were overruled.

Plans were being developed for the nuclear bombing of Japan even as the Trinity test was being planned. B-29 bombers were modified to carry the new weapon. Crews were chosen and specially trained for the mission, but they were not told until the very last minute what sort of

"Fat Man" specifications (MPHPA)

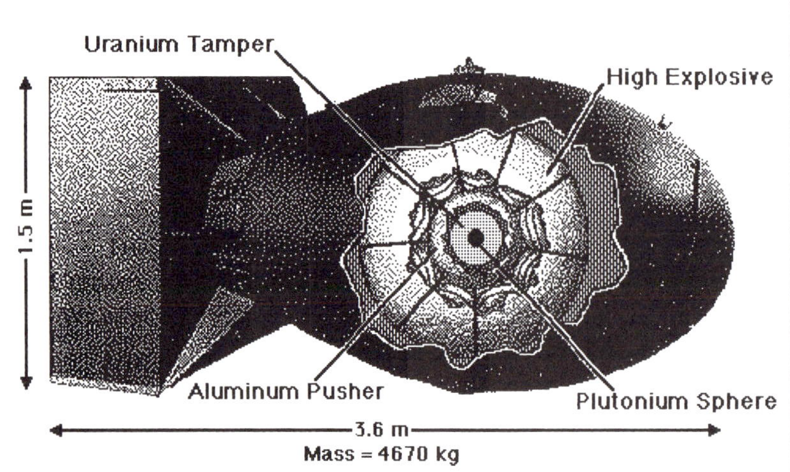

"Fat Man"

Weight: 10,800 lbs

Length: 10 ft 8 in.; Diameter: 60 in.

Enriched Plutonium Fuel: 13.6 lbs; approx. size of a softball – Produced at Hanford, WA

Plutonium core surrounded by 5,300 lbs of high explosives; plutonium core reduced to size of tennis ball

Bomb Initiator: Beryllium - Polonium (Neutron Source)

Approx 1.176 Kilograms of plutonium converted to energy

Explosive force: 21,000 tons of TNT equivalent

Use: Dropped on Japanese city of Nagasaki; August 9, 1945

Nuclear Weaponeer: Navy Cdr. Frederick Ashworth

Delivery: B-29 "Bockscar" piloted by Maj. Charles Sweeney

Firebombing raid over Japan, July 1945 (MPHPA)

weapon they were to drop. The plan called for the uranium "Little Boy" bomb to be dropped first, followed by the plutonium "Fat Man" bomb on a second target. As many plutonium bombs as necessary were to be manufactured and used to force the surrender of Japan. There were daily deliveries of bomb-making material to Tinian, transforming the island into the world's largest air base.

Japan's home islands had been devastated by American bombing raids directed by General Curtis LeMay. On some missions, one thousand B-29 Superfortress bombers took off in fifteen-second intervals from six ten-lane runways to bomb targets in Japan. During ten days in March, 11,600 B-29 sorties had wiped out thirty-two square miles of the four largest Japanese cities, killing more than 150,000 people and leaving a million more homeless. By mid-1945, saturation bombing had devastated most of Japan's major cities. Houses built of wood and rice paper would go up like matchsticks in the firestorms created by the bombing. Thousands of civilians were killed in these raids. One raid in Tokyo on May 25 sparked a massive firestorm that swept through the city. Bomber crews claimed they could smell burning flesh thousands of feet below. Indeed, the bombings were so thorough that General Groves was hard-pressed to find a suitable target for "Little Boy."

Secretary of War Stimson was appalled when he heard of LeMay's devastating May 25 raid on Tokyo. Stimson was an old-school gentleman who believed in "civilized" war with rules of fair play. He had insisted on "precision" bombing to limit destruction to military targets and minimize civilian casualties. Several days after the Tokyo raid, Stimson called Groves and demanded to know the target list for the A-bomb. Groves grudgingly told him the target was Kyoto. Stimson was horrified. Kyoto was the cradle of Japanese civilization—the cultural, intellectual, and spiritual center of Japan. Stimson, who had once visited the ancient Buddhist and Shinto shrines in the city, ordered Groves not to bomb Kyoto.

A target committee selected a new list of potential targets for the atomic bomb—Hiroshima, Kokura, Niigata, and Nagasaki. Hiroshima was at the top of the list. It was an attractive target because it had a large military depot and an industrial area, and it was surrounded by hills, which would focus the power of the bomb blast. It was also the only one of the potential target cities that did not contain an Allied prisoner-of-war camp. Located on Hiroshima Bay and capital of the Hiroshima Prefecture, the city was home to approximately 320,000 people in 1945. And unlike Tokyo and other major Japanese cities that had been devastated by frequent bombing raids, Hiroshima had so far been spared such destruction; it remained almost totally unscathed. The pristine condition of Hiroshima made it an appealing target to the military because it would be easier to assess the total destructive power of the atomic bomb.

A mosaic view of Hiroshima, April 13, 1945, months before the attack (National Archives)

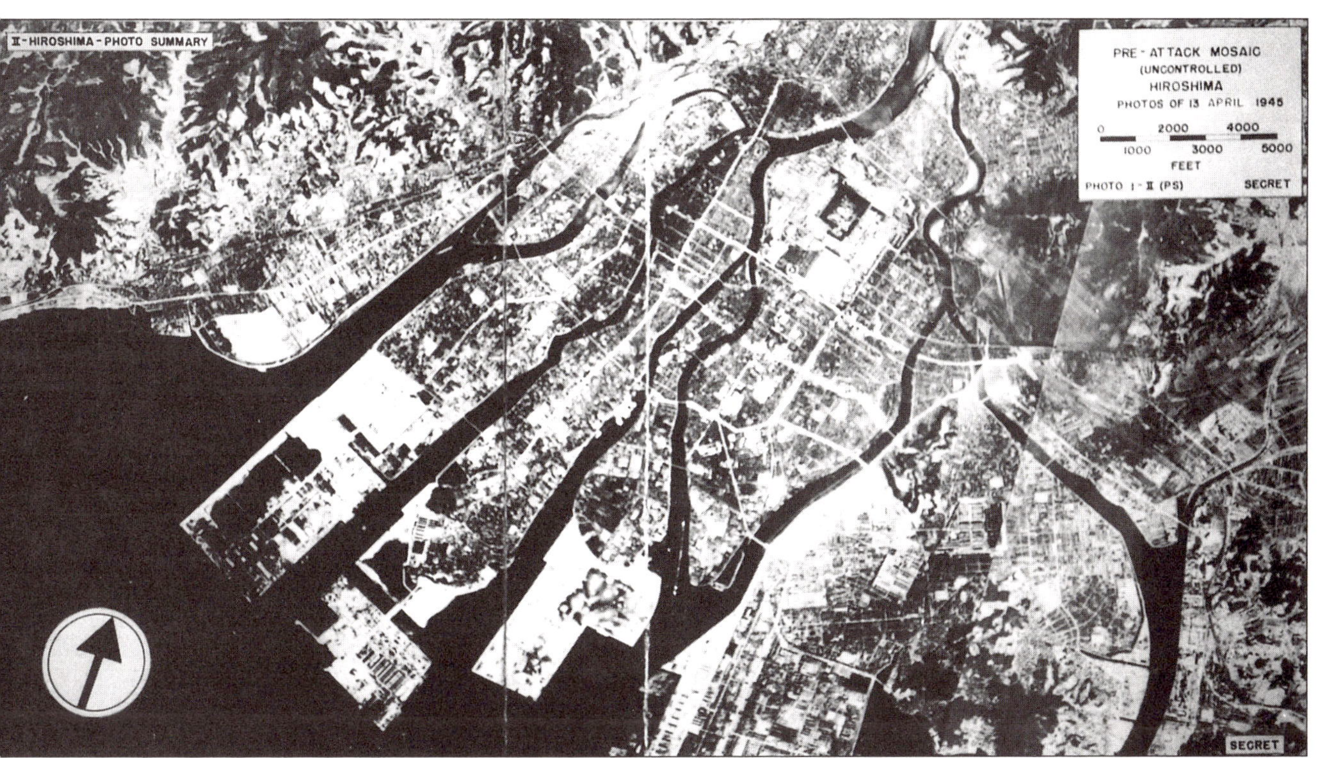

Eight
Rain of Ruin

It seemed the end of the world.
—Tatsuichiro Akizuki, Physician and Nagasaki Survivor 1945

Commanding Special Bombing Mission No. 13 was Lieutenant Colonel Paul W. Tibbets of the 509th Composite Group. The 509th had been activated in December 1944. The mission of this self-sustaining unit was to train and prepare for dropping the atomic bomb. A seasoned, highly respected bomber pilot, twenty-nine-year-old Lieutenant Colonel Tibbets was a veteran of twenty-five combat missions in Europe and North Africa in which he piloted the B-17 Flying Fortress. He also served as a test pilot for the B-29 bomber, which made him well acquainted with its characteristics and idiosyncrasies. Tibbets was chosen to head the 509th because he was a superb officer. Groves, however, had doubts about Tibbets. He acknowledged his ability as a pilot, but Groves thought Tibbets too young to effectively head the group.

Tibbets had carte blanche in choosing personnel for the 509th. He selected men he had flown with in Europe and North Africa and in the B-29 test program. He kept the crews he selected together. He was forbidden to tell them the true nature of their assignment. All he was at liberty to say was that they would be engaged in a top-secret project that, if successful, would end the war as much as twelve months sooner than anticipated.

The bombing mission involved three aircraft. Carrying the bomb would be Aircraft 44-86292, a B-29 bomber specially modified for the mission that Tibbets christened *Enola Gay* in honor of his mother. Accompanying the *Enola Gay* were two B-29 escorts, the unnamed No. 91 piloted by Major George Marquardt and *The Great Artiste* piloted by Major Charles Sweeney. Stationed on Iwo Jima was a standby plane, Captain Charles McKnight's *Top Secret*. Scouting the weather ahead were the *Jabbit III* flying over Kokura, *Full House* at Nagasaki, and *Straight Flush* at Hiroshima.

Enola Gay *crew members, including the ground crew (MPHPA)*

On August 4, 1945, Tibbets called together the crews of the *Enola Gay* and the two escort planes on Tinian for a final mission briefing. One of General Groves's deputies, Captain William "Deak" Parsons, told them: "The bomb you are going to drop is something new in the history of warfare. It is the most destructive weapon ever produced. We think it will knock out almost everything within a three-mile radius." This startling introduction was followed with a film of the Trinity blast, but the projector broke down and started chewing up the film. Parsons stepped in to describe in vivid detail what had happened at Trinity. The men were stunned. They could not comprehend a weapon of such awesome power. Even at this late date, Parsons avoided using the words *atomic* or *nuclear,* but he did warn the pilots that under no circumstances were they to fly through the mushroom cloud. It would contain high, potentially lethal levels of radioactivity. Now the pilots understood why they had been practicing steep, breakaway turns during the mission training.

After Parsons finished his briefing, he handed the meeting over to an air-rescue specialist. This operation was the most closely supported mission in history. Hundreds of planes, ships, and submarines would patrol off the coast of Japan ready to rescue any crews of planes that had to ditch in the ocean. If captured, the crew members were to give only their name, rank, serial number, and date of birth. Tibbets was secretly issued a box of cyanide tablets for his crew with orders that they kill themselves in the event of capture to avoid interrogation. Tibbets wisely decided to keep this to himself unless capture was imminent.

On August 6, 1945, at 2:45 A.M., *Enola Gay* rolled down the runway on Tinian and took off for Japan. Over Iwo Jima, *Enola Gay* formed up in a loose V formation with her escorts. The original plan called for the

"Little Boy" on trailer cradle in pit (National Archives)

bomb to be fully armed at takeoff, but Parsons feared that if anything happened to the plane, it could trigger a nuclear explosion that would blow up half of Tinian. He ordered the bomb to be armed after takeoff. It was only after the *Enola Gay* had been flying toward Japan for several hours and the bomb had been armed that Tibbets announced to his crew, "We are carrying the world's first atomic bomb."

Tibbets received word that the weather was good over all three potential targets. He switched on the intercom and announced to the crew: "It's Hiroshima." The bomb bay doors of the *Enola Gay* opened over Hiroshima at 8:15 A.M., Tinian time, and "Little Boy" dropped toward its target. Suddenly lightened of its nine-thousand-pound load, the plane lurched upward. There was what seemed like a long delay and then a flash of bright light filled the plane, and a shockwave rattled it. A second shockwave followed. Tibbets radioed Tinian: "Target visually bombed with good results." The copilot, keeping his own notes, had a more emotional response. He wrote, "My God, what have we done?"

President Truman was at sea on board the cruiser *Augusta*, returning from his trip to Potsdam, when he received news of the bombing. "This is the greatest day in history," he proclaimed. Groves phoned Oppenheimer at Los Alamos with the news. Oppenheimer did not share Truman's exultation, but he was pleased with the results. Anne Wilson, Oppenheimer's secretary, recalled that when the announcement went over the intercom, "The place went up like we'd won the Army-Navy game." As he entered the auditorium to speak to his staff, Oppenheimer was greeted with triumphant cheers. When he reached the podium, Oppenheimer clasped his hands above his head, posed like a victorious prizefighter.

President Harry S Truman made the final decision on whether or not to use the atomic bomb against Japan. (Library of Congress)

Smoke billowed 20,000 feet above Hiroshima after the bomb exploded. (National Archives)

The Japanese had no idea what was used against Hiroshima. Their official radio broadcast announced: "Hiroshima suffered considerable damage as the result of an attack by a few B-29s. It is believed that a new type of bomb was used. The details are being investigated." A Japanese general sent to investigate reported the following:

> There was but one black dead tree, as if a crow was perched on it. There was nothing there but that tree. As we landed at the airport all the grass was red as if it had been toasted. . . . Everything had burned up simultaneously. Some schools with blown-off roofs and broken windows were left standing at some distance from the center of the city. But the city itself was completely wiped out. That must be the word, yes, completely wiped out.

A post-attack mosaic view of Hiroshima, August 11, 1945 (National Archives)

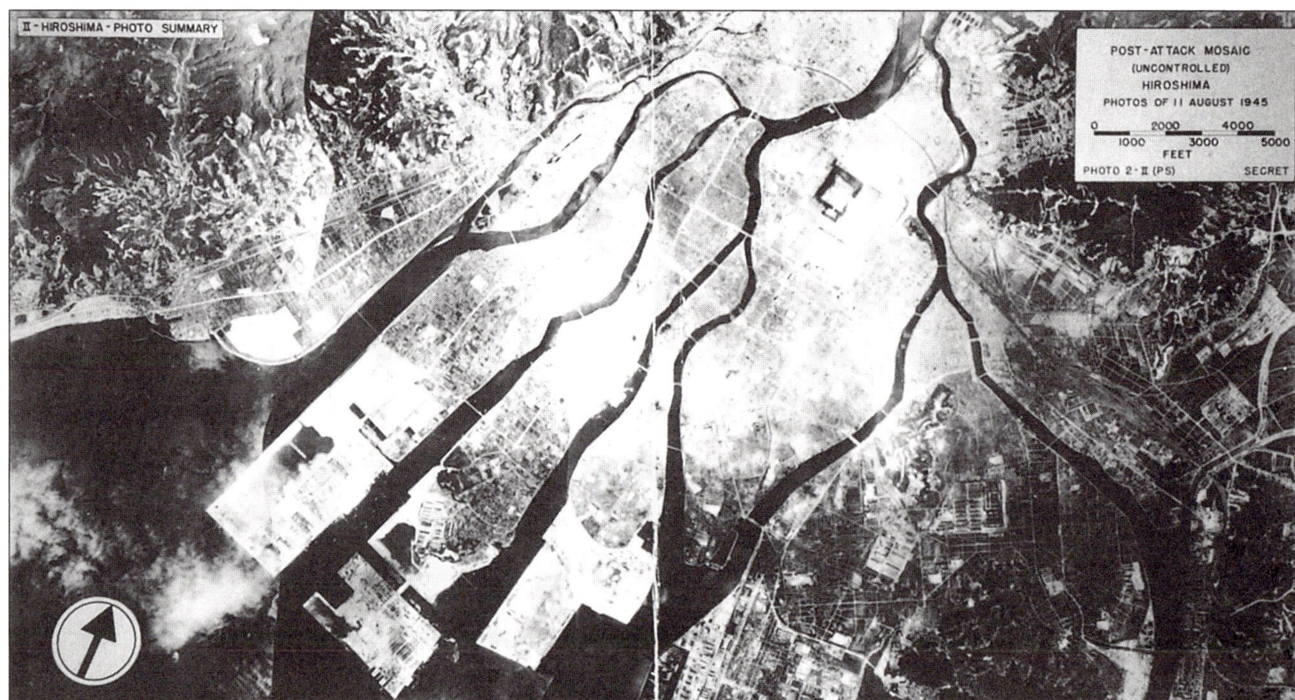

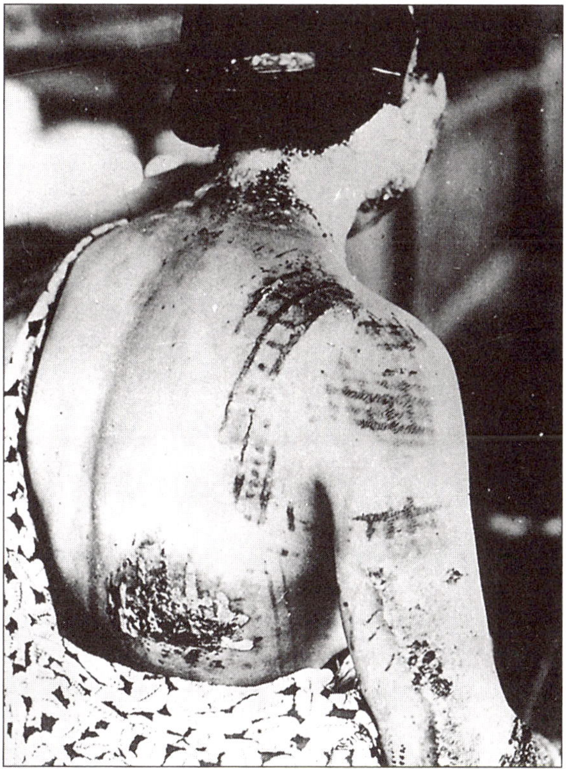

The skin of this atomic bomb survivor is burned in a pattern corresponding to the dark portions of the kimono she wore at the time of the explosion. Many survivors suffered similar burn patterns. (National Archives)

Ninety percent of the city was destroyed. Fires burned for days because all the firefighters had been killed in the blast and their equipment destroyed. Most of the hospitals were decimated, and the few surviving doctors and nurses were overwhelmed with injured victims. The scant medical supplies they had were quickly exhausted. Getting in and out of the city was impossible. Railways were wiped out and streets, strewn with rubble from collapsed buildings, were impassable. Communication with the outside world was nonexistent—all telegraph and telephone lines had been destroyed. Naomi Shohno, who lost her family and later became a nuclear physicist, recorded how survivors tried to cope with the devastation:

> All buildings such as shrines, factories, and barracks, not to mention schools that had already been designated as refuges and the hospitals that remained unburned, were used as temporary relief camps. Most buildings in the city, even if their superstructures remained intact, were half-

The wrecked framework of the Museum of Science and Industry in Hiroshima as it appeared shortly after the bombing (Library of Congress)

destroyed, with their windowpanes and walls blown out and a heap of debris lying scattered on the floor. Medical treatment was most difficult, because many doctors and nurses were injured—in Hiroshima, for example, 90 percent of its doctors (270) and 93 percent of its nurses (1,650) suffered death or injury in the bombing—and medical supplies and equipment had been destroyed.

The death and devastation were so overwhelming to survivors that they were unable to cope with anything other than their own needs. Cries of the injured were ignored as people rushed by to escape fires, seek help for their own injuries, or search for loved ones.

Immediately following the Hiroshima bombing, American planes dropped leaflets throughout Japan warning the Japanese of impending doom if they chose to continue the war. Leaflet #1 read:

> When one's home appears to be falling, one does not run away. Rather one repairs the bad places.
>
> Japan is now facing a crisis. In other words, the Army is the source of decay within your country. That the Army is deceiving you regarding their strength is evidenced by the air raids that you have experienced recently. Remove your war leaders and save your country!

Leaflet #2 read:

> People of Japan!
>
> A message from President Harry S Truman of the United States of America.
>
> Nazi Germany has been destroyed. You citizens of Japan will be made aware of the tremendous offensive might of the combined land, sea and air forces of the United States. As long as your government officials and military leaders persist in their war efforts we will increase our offensive posture and destroy all facilities that provide support for your armed forces. Prolonging this war will only increase the suffering of the people. There is nothing to be gained for the people. However, we will continue our offensive until the Japanese army throws down its weapons and surrenders unconditionally. Surrender will destroy the power of the military leaders who have brought the Japanese people to the brink of disaster and untold suffering to the soldiers and sailors whom you love. Surrender will also permit them to return to their farms and workplaces. Surrender WILL NOT mean a life of slavery for you.

Leaflet #3 read:

> You can understand the frightening reality by seeing the destruction caused in Hiroshima by one bomb.
>
> The United States hopes that you will plead with the Emperor to end this war so that it will not be necessary to use many atomic bombs.
>
> The President of the United States hopes that the thirteen articles [referring to the Potsdam Declaration calling for Japan's unconditional surrender] will be approved quickly and that peace can come to the new Japan.
>
> You must suspend armed opposition immediately. Otherwise, the United States will use the atom bomb in addition to the superior weapons available to permanently end this war.
>
> Evacuate the cities immediately!

The hope was that this propaganda would encourage the Japanese people to rise up against the army and their emperor and make demands for peace that could not be refused. The effectiveness of the leaflets would never be known. Seventy-five hours after "Little Boy" was dropped on Hiroshima, Nagasaki became the second city to be attacked with an atomic weapon.

Special Bombing Mission No. 16 was originally scheduled for August 11, but forecasts of bad weather accelerated the date. On August 9, another B-29 bomber, *Bockscar* (also spelled *Bock's Car* in some accounts) named after Captain Frederick Bock and piloted by Major Charles Sweeney, dropped the plutonium bomb "Fat Man" on Nagasaki, an industrial seaport city with a population of approximately 240,000. "Fat Man," a bulbous five-ton weapon, was a duplicate of "the Gadget." It was a more complex weapon than "Little Boy," so much so that it had to be armed before takeoff. The weather was poor at Tinian the morning *Bockscar* was to fly its mission, making flying conditions hazardous. Norman Ramsey, charged with arming "Fat Man," feared the plane would crash on takeoff and vaporize the entire island. Ramsey stationed himself at the end of the runway to watch *Bockscar* take off. He breathed a sigh of relief at 3:49 A.M. when the plane lifted off the runway and headed for its target.

Bockscar was not as lucky as *Enola Gay*—the weather was bad and was expected to get worse. After making three runs and wasting forty-five minutes and precious fuel flying over the primary target, Kokura, Sweeney changed course and headed for the secondary target, Nagasaki. He computed he had enough fuel for only one attempt. *Bockscar* encountered a thick, overcast sky over Nagasaki. Sweeney violated orders and used radar for his approach. Only at the very last moment was there a break in the clouds, permitting a visual bombing. "Fat Man" exploded in midair one thousand six hundred feet above Nagasaki, killing approximately forty thousand people. Tatsuichiro Akizuki, a physician working at the Urakami Hospital in Nagasaki, recorded in his diary the devastation he witnessed:

> All the buildings I could see were on fire. . . . Electricity poles were wrapped in flame like so many pieces of kindling. Trees on nearby hills were smoking, as were the leaves of sweet potatoes in fields. . . . It seemed as if the earth itself emitted fire and smoke, flames that writhed up and erupted from the underground. The sky was dark, the ground was scarlet, and in between hung clouds of yellowish smoke. Three kinds of color—black, yellow, and scarlet—loomed ominously over the people, who ran about like so many ants seeking escape . . . that ocean of fire, that sky of smoke! It seemed the end of the world.

Survivors moving along a road after the bombing of Nagasaki (National Archives)

Bockscar made it back to the secondary landing field in Okinawa with its fuel exhausted—the plane was literally flying on fumes. There was not enough gas for Sweeney to even taxi the plane off the runway.

Hanford and Oak Ridge were still producing plutonium and uranium, and Los Alamos was still assembling bombs. The core for the third bomb, destined for Tinian, was intercepted at the last moment in Los Alamos. Reports from Tokyo suggested that the Japanese were considering unconditional surrender. Groves and General Marshall decided

A mushroom cloud rising over Nagasaki (Library of Congress)

The Hanford Engineer Works in Richland, Washington
(Library of Congress)

to hold off on further shipments to Tinian. If the Japanese did not surrender by August 13, shipments would resume.

Despite the horrific reports coming from Hiroshima and Nagasaki, the members of the Japanese Inner Cabinet could not bring themselves to surrender. They debated late into the evening of August 9. There were millions of Japanese soldiers who were barely tested in battle and still eager to fight. They might not surrender even if ordered to do so. Desperate to break the deadlock, Premier Kantaro Suzuki suggested that Emperor Hirohito might help them come to a decision. Suzuki's suggestion broke the long-standing Japanese tradition against imperial intervention in government affairs—only unanimous recommendations from the cabinet were supposed to be brought before the emperor.

Emperor Hirohito of Japan posing in dress uniform (Library of Congress)

Oak Ridgers in Jackson Square hanging Japanese Prime Minister Tojo in effigy on V-J (Victory in Japan) Day (U.S. Department of Energy)

A tired and worried Hirohito met with the cabinet ten minutes before midnight. For over two hours, old arguments against surrender that deadlocked previous meetings were repeated, but the emperor was determined to break the stalemate. A third atomic bomb could fall at any moment. There was a rumor that Tokyo would be bombed on August 12. Premier Suzuki invited the emperor to express his wishes. The emperor rose and in a voice strained with emotion said: "I cannot bear to see my innocent people suffer any longer. Ending the war is the only way to restore world peace and to relieve the nation from the terrible distress with which it is burdened." He paid tribute to all who had fallen in battle and at home. He wiped tears from his cheeks with white-gloved hands. Everyone in the conference room sobbed uncon-

Celebratory Oak Ridgers holding copies of The Knoxville Journal *announcing the unconditional surrender of Japan and the end of World War II (U.S. Department of Energy)*

trollably. "The time has come when we must bear the unbearable," he said, and left the conference.

The leaders responded to the emperor's command and approved acceptance of the Potsdam Declaration, which called for unconditional surrender. There was still, however, resistance to surrender among the army and militant cabinet members. The War Ministry released the statement: "We are determined to fight resolutely, although we may have to chew grass, eat dirt and sleep in fields." A group of army staff officers planned a coup. They would surround the emperor's palace with local troops, occupy crucial government buildings, take control of the press and radio, and cut off communications. The plan was abandoned when senior officers refused to support it. The emperor asserted himself again and summoned another imperial conference with his cabinet. Wiping tears from his face, he said in a quaking voice: "I wish to save the people at the risk of my own life. I am ready to do anything. If it is for the good of the people, I am willing to make a broadcast." On August 15 the Japanese people heard their emperor's voice for the first time. In a recorded message, Emperor Hirohito announced on the radio the government's unconditional surrender to the Allied powers.

> The enemy has begun to employ a new and most cruel bomb, the power of which to do damage is indeed incalculable, taking the toll of many innocent lives. Should we continue to fight it would not only result in an ultimate collapse and obliteration of the Japanese nation, but also it would lead to the total extinction of human civilization. . . .

World War II had finally come to an end.

The August 15, 1945, issue of The Washington Post. *The second headline announces the loss of the USS* Indianapolis. *(Library of Congress)*

The Weather

Today—Brief showers and cooler but some sunshine. Highest temperature in the low 80's. Yesterday—High, 87; low 73. (Details on Page 14)

The Washington Post

Single Copy Price 5c

NO. 25,262 WASHINGTON: WEDNESDAY, AUGUST 15, 1945

HISTORY'S WORST WAR IS OVER!

Cruiser Indianapolis Sunk, 883 Lost

2 Torpedoes Send U. S. Ship Down in Few Minutes

Search Plane Leads To Belated Rescue Of 315 Survivors in Philippines Sea

By Morrie Landsberg

Peleliu, Palau Islands, Aug. 5 (Delayed) (AP).—The 10,000-ton cruiser Indianapolis was sunk in less than 15 minutes, presumably by a Japanese submarine, 12 minutes past midnight July 30—and 883 crew members lost their lives in one of the Navy's worst disasters. The cruiser had just speeded an atomic bomb from San Francisco to the Marianas.

She went down in the Philippines Sea, within 450 miles of Leyte while on an unescorted high speed run from San Francisco.

The fatal torpedo attack came without a second's warning. Two

Cheering, Milling Crowd In Downtown Victory Celebration

Cut in Draft To 50,000 Monthly Set

Manpower Controls End, Giving Nation Free Labor Market, First Time in 2 Years

Some Controls Kept

RECONVERSION speeded up; some controls to be kept by WPB. Page 5.

Truman Acts Quickly

By James E. Chinn

Orders for immediate reduction in draft calls from 80,000 to 50,000 a month, and lifting of all manpower controls which gives the Nation a free labor market for the first time in more than two years, came last night hard on the heels of President Truman's official announcement of Japan's surrender.

Simultaneously, the President disclosed plans for a stepped-up program for release of veterans, and predicted that between 5 and 5½ million men now in the Army may be returned to civilian life in the next 12 to 18 months.

The cut in draft calls will halt induction of men 26 and over. Of the 50,000 under that age to be inducted each month, a majority will be boys reaching 18. The post-war draftees will serve as replacements and support the forces required for occupation duty.

Japan Accepts Declaration Of Potsdam Without Change; MacArthur Will Rule With Hirohito As His Mouthpiece

By Edward T. Folliard

The war is over!

The victory of the United States and its Allies is complete and overwhelming. It has come according to the grand strategic plan: Germany first and then Japan. Nowhere on earth now—unless it be by mistake—are troops shooting to kill.

President Truman, standing behind his desk at the White House, made the historic announcement at 7 o'clock last evening. He said that Japan had accepted the Allies' Potsdam Declaration calling for unconditional surrender. He said that in the Japanese note of acceptance there was "no qualification."

For the first time in history an island world power had capitulated without an invasion. Last night a Tokyo broadcast gave the reason. It quoted Emperor Hirohito as saying that Japan had decided to get out of the war because of the atomic bomb.

President Truman, a tanned, smiling figure in blue suit, blue shirt and blue-and-white tie, took less than five minutes to give out the news for which the whole world was waiting. The fateful words came at the very outset:

"I have received this afternoon a message from the Japanese Government in reply to the message forwarded to that government by the Secretary of State on August 11.

They Shall Not Have Died in Vain

1941 Dec. 7th. 1942

Remember PEARL HARBOR

WORK

FIGHT

SACRIFICE

Let's get it over with!

COME ON, C-H... DO MORE!

THIS ISN'T PEACE-IT'S WAR!!

Nine
Aftermath

It wasn't necessary to hit them with that awful thing.
—General Dwight D. Eisenhower,
Supreme Allied Forces Commander, European Theater

"Little Boy" and "Fat Man" killed approximately 150,000 people outright and injured another 125,000. Within five months another 60,000 people had died from their injuries or from radiation sickness. Within five years 275,000 people had died as a direct result of the atomic bombs. Pope Pius XII sent a formal protest to President Truman lamenting the lack of immunity for civilian populations. Einstein told a *New York Times* reporter who called him at home, "The world is not yet ready for it." A telegram sent to President Truman from the Federal Council of Churches of Christ in America opposed further use of the weapon. Truman's unapologetic reply reflected the sentiments popular with the majority of Americans.

> Nobody is more disturbed over the use of the atomic bomb than I am, but I was greatly disturbed over the unwarranted attack by the Japanese on Pearl Harbor and their murder of our prisoners of war.

"Remember Pearl Harbor" was a phrase used throughout World War II to rally people on the home front. (National Archives)

A "Stay on the Job" rally in Oak Ridge (U.S. Department of Energy)

For most Americans, the news of the atomic bomb being used against Japan to force surrender was welcome. Americans still held plenty of animosity against the Japanese. A poll taken shortly before the bombing revealed that one-third of Americans wanted Emperor Hirohito executed as a war criminal.

General Marshall warned General Groves against greeting the bombings with "too much gratification" because so many Japanese had been killed, but Groves expressed popular American sentiments when he curtly replied that he was not thinking so much about the Japanese casualties "as I was about the men who made the Bataan Death March." That event and others, like the devastating sneak attack against Pearl Harbor, were still fresh and vivid in the minds of most Americans, making it difficult for them to feel sympathy for the thousands of Japanese killed in the bombings.

The soldiers who would have had to storm the shores of Japan's home islands in the invasion greeted the news of the bombings with elation. Evan Thomas writes in a 1995 *Newsweek* article:

> In August 1945, the GIs waiting to invade Japan had no doubt about the wisdom of obliterating Hiroshima and Nagasaki with nuclear weapons. Upon hearing the news, "we whooped and yelled like mad, we downed all the beer we'd been stashing away," one dogface later recalled. . . . Paul Fussel, a 21-year-old second lieutenant leading a rifle platoon, remembered that "for all the fake manliness of our facades, we cried with relief and joy. We were actually going to live. We were going to grow up after all."

Back in the United States, the millions of parents, friends, wives, children, and sweethearts of those soldiers shared their loved ones' joy. They, too, did not question the decision to bomb Japan.

Workers in Hanford and Oak Ridge did not hear the news of Hiroshima and Nagasaki or the surrender of Japan before anyone else in the country, but the news was probably greeted with more jubilation in those places than elsewhere. The bombings were stunning revelations to the thousands of workers in Hanford and Oak Ridge who had labored seven days a week for three years on a project they knew very little about. They were told the work they were doing was vital to the war effort and were put under enormous, continuous pressure to complete it. Leon Overstreet, a construction worker in Hanford, recalls:

> We worked overtime nearly all the time, probably 10 hours a day. . . . Most of the time we worked six days, they were in a hurry. Sometimes we worked on Sunday. I was making $1.65 an hour, but that was the wages then. . . . When we heard about the bombs, it was a great feeling. I felt that my efforts had been worthwhile. Everybody I worked with was glad to be a part of it. That ended the war, and saved a lot of lives.

The initial reaction of the workers to the news of the bombings was one of disbelief. It was difficult to fathom the awesome destructive power of a nuclear bomb. By the afternoon, horns, whistles, and anything else that could make noise were sounding in celebration at all the project sites. People left their homes and jobs and gathered together to celebrate and buy every newspaper that carried the story. June Adamson describes the atmosphere in Oak Ridge following the announcement of the Hiroshima bombing:

> Excitement. We couldn't believe it. The secret was out at last, and we couldn't wait to share it. Goose flesh made us shiver even on this hot day. There were moments of deep concern, a feeling of awe at the power released. But there was pride, too, even exaltation, relief, celebration.

The *Oak Ridge Journal,* published weekly every Thursday, did not rush out an extra, but its August 9, 1945, edition did carry the banner headline: OAK RIDGE ATTACKS JAPANESE. Extras of regional newspapers sold out faster than they could be printed. June Adamson recalls:

> In front of the post office on Tennessee Avenue, extra editions of area newspapers were being sold. Later in the day, newsboys were swarming up and down the streets, an unheard of practice previously in the secret city. Headlines read: "Power of Oak Ridge Atomic Bomb Hits Japan: Truman Reveals Use of World's Greatest Bomb; World's Biggest, Best Kept Secret Hidden at CEW; Atomic Super Bomb Made at Oak Ridge

> Strikes Japan; Story of Secret City Officially Told; 20,000 Ton Atom Smashes Japan; Allies Tell Japs Hirohito Must Obey Our Commands; Bomb Staggers Nips."

"Japs" and "Nips" were derogatory names for the Japanese used throughout the war. Extras of the Knoxville newspapers sold for a dollar a copy. One man sold one thousand six hundred newspapers in thirty-five minutes.

The astonishing naïveté among the public at large about the atomic bomb was reflected in the letters that flooded the offices of Oak Ridge officials in the days following the Hiroshima bombing. In one letter

Boys at Oak Ridge in a model airplane they called The Atom *(U.S. Department of Energy)*

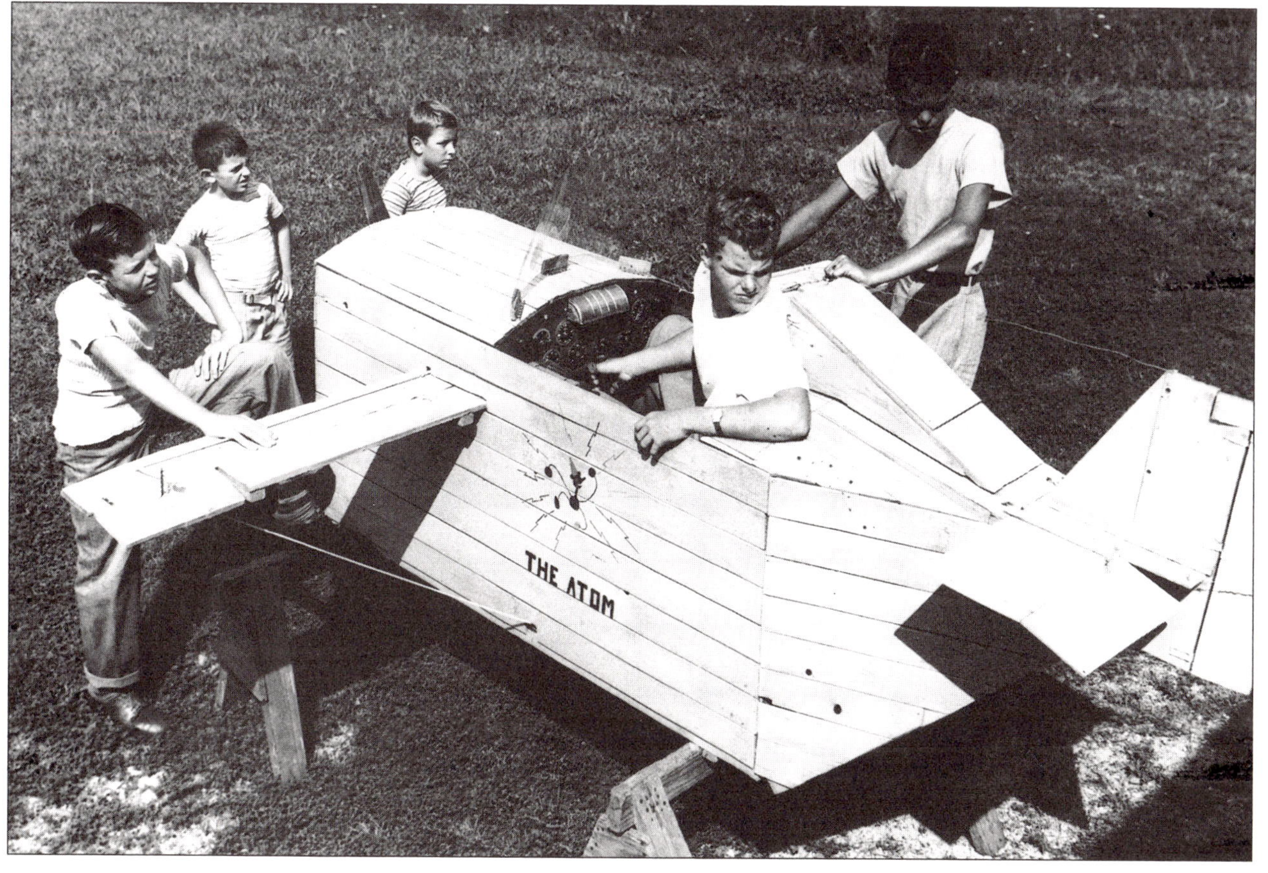

addressed to the "Atomic Bomb Company" of Oak Ridge, an Arkansas man asked to purchase some atomic bombs to blow tree stumps out of his field. Companies wanted to associate their products with the Manhattan Project. A laundry equipment supplier requested permission to advertise that its machines had been used in the townsite laundry. Merita wanted to advertise that its bread was the only bread distributed at Oak Ridge. Everyone wanted to say they had played some small part in the success of the project.

There was, however, considerable dissent over the use of the atomic bombs. General Dwight Eisenhower, supreme commander of the European theater who led Allied forces to defeat Germany and would later succeed Truman as president of the United States, said this:

> I voiced to Secretary of War Stimson my grave misgivings, first on the basis of my belief that Japan was already defeated and that dropping the bomb was completely unnecessary, and secondly because I thought that our country should avoid shocking world opinion by the use of the weapon whose employment was, I thought, no longer mandatory as a measure to save American lives. It was my belief that Japan was, at this very moment, seeking a way to surrender with a minimum loss of "face" [honor].

Admiral Leahy, chairman of the Joint Chiefs of Staff during World War II, was more damning in his criticism.

> The use of this barbarous weapon at Hiroshima and Nagasaki was not of material assistance in our war against Japan. The Japanese were already defeated and ready to surrender. . . .

The division among the project scientists in their views on dropping the bombs continued after the war. Einstein, whose participation in the Manhattan Project was limited but extremely influential, deeply regretted his actions for the rest of his life. In 1946 he remarked: "If I had known that the Germans would not succeed in constructing the bomb, I would never have lifted a finger."

Yet Glenn Seaborg, a physicist who worked on producing plutonium at Hanford, was proud of the achievement: "The Manhattan Project was probably the most important, certainly the most exciting, thing I ever did." At a speaking engagement in Geneva, Switzerland, many years after the war, a Jesuit priest in the audience asked Oppenheimer if he would do it all over again given the choice. Without hesitation, Oppenheimer replied yes. He would later reflect:

> I have no remorse about the making of the bomb and Trinity. That was done right. As for how we used it, I understand why it happened and appreciate with what nobility those with whom I'd worked made their decision. But I do not have the feeling that it was done right. . . . Our government should have acted with more foresight and clarity in telling the world and Japan what the bomb meant.

Physicist Edward Teller, who all along advocated for bigger, more powerful bombs and would soon become known as "Father of the Hydrogen Bomb," was least repentant among the Manhattan Project scientists.

> I have been asked again and again, if I have regrets. Will you please excuse me, this is one of the most idiotic questions, except for the fact that apparently others do have regrets. I didn't put the world together and if you had the choice that something simple that was in the long run unavoidable should be first done by the United States or the Nazis or by the Soviets or by someone else, would you have regrets to make sure we did it first?

President Truman remained silent about his decision to drop the bombs for nearly twenty years. In February 1965 the former president, who had kept on his desk in the Oval Office a plaque that read THE BUCK STOPS HERE, said this in a television interview:

> It was a question of saving hundreds of thousands of American lives. I don't mind telling you that you don't feel normal when you have to plan hundreds of thousands of complete final deaths of American boys who are alive and joking and having fun while you are doing your planning. You break your heart and your head trying to figure a way to save one life. . . . I could not worry about what history would say about my personal morality. I made the only decision I ever knew how to make. I did what I thought was right.

The debate over the military and moral justifications of the bombings of Hiroshima and Nagasaki continues to this day. Just as opinion was and continues to be divided among historians, military leaders, politicians, and scientists, so it is among the rest of Americans. The bombing of Hiroshima may seem more excusable to some Americans because many believe it saved untold numbers of American and Japanese lives. The bombing of Nagasaki, however, poses a more perplexing ethical question, even for those who endorse the Hiroshima bombing. Was the bombing of Nagasaki a needless act of cruelty? Was it fair for the United States to have allowed only three days for the Japanese to respond to Hiroshima? It took the stunned Japanese considerable time to comprehend and evaluate the devastation of the weapon. They also had to face in that short span of time the decision of unconditional surrender. If the Japanese had been given more time to assess and respond to the situation, the bombing of Nagasaki might not have been necessary.

There was an appalling callousness in the decision to drop the second bomb on Japan. There was no discussion or debate among military and political authorities about whether a second bomb attack was necessary. General Groves recalled: "There was never any decision reached to drop *only* two bombs. As far as I was concerned, there was no limit to the number of bombs that would be used. There was no debate ever on the matter of dropping a second bomb. The debate had all been on whether to use the atomic bomb as a weapon at all." A third bomb would certainly have been used against another city had Japan not capitulated.

President Truman, General Groves, and other advocates for using the bomb justified the attacks on Hiroshima and Nagasaki with the argument that the bombings saved the lives of hundreds of thousands of Americans and millions of Japanese who would have died in an invasion of Japan's home islands. Another pressing concern was the Soviet Union's declaration of war against Japan on August 8. A 1946 study by the U.S. Strategic Bombing Survey found: "Certainly prior to 31 December 1945, and in all probability prior to 1 November 1945, Japan would have surrendered even if the atomic bombs had not been dropped . . . and even if no invasion or plan had been contemplated." J. Samuel Walker, historian for the U.S. Nuclear Regulatory Commission, argued: "The consensus among scholars is that the bomb was not needed to avoid an invasion of Japan. . . . It is clear that alternatives to the bomb existed and that Truman and his advisors knew it."

If President Truman had indeed been aware of all the alternatives, why did he decide to drop the bomb? Was he dutifully honoring what he thought was President Roosevelt's desire to use the bomb against Japan? Some historians suggest that the decision was beyond Truman, that there was too much momentum at that point in history not to use the bomb. Perhaps Truman was doing what he believed the majority of

Americans wanted, revenge for Pearl Harbor and atrocities like the Bataan Death March, or perhaps Truman really did believe that dropping the bomb was the best alternative for ending the war with Japan.

Almost a half century later, passions on both sides of the debate ran high over the Smithsonian Institution's plans to mount an exhibit commemorating the fiftieth anniversary of the flight of the *Enola Gay.* The National Air and Space Museum planned to exhibit the *Enola Gay,* including in it broken and burned artifacts and photographs of victims and survivors from Hiroshima and Nagasaki. Veterans groups such as the Air Force Association strongly objected to the inclusion of these artifacts, charging the exhibit was politically biased and would distort the historical context of the atomic bombing of Japan. The controversy received international attention and kicked off a political firestorm, with some members of Congress going so far as threatening to withhold funding from the museum. Angry veterans' groups accused these historical "revisionists" of encouraging the exhibit curators to let political correctness run amok by depicting the Japanese as innocent victims. Paul Tibbets said this about the controversy:

> From my point of view, the matter has been politicized, and, as a result, mishandled . . . history has been denigrated; the *Enola Gay* has been miscast and a group of valiant Americans have had their role in history treated shamefully. . . . In 1945, I was wearing the uniform of the U.S. Army [Air Forces] following the orders of our commander-in-chief. I was, to the best of my ability, doing what I could to bring the war to victorious conclusion—just as millions of people were doing here at home and around the world. . . . During the course of the half century that has elapsed since the use of the atomic weapons, many scribes have chronicled the flight of the *Enola Gay* with nothing but descriptions of the destructive nature of our atomic weapons. . . . Most writers have looked

> to the ashes of Hiroshima and Nagasaki to find answers for the use of those atomic weapons. The real answers lay in thousands of graves from Pearl Harbor around the world to Normandy and back again.

In response to the widely publicized controversy, the Smithsonian curators drastically scaled down the fiftieth anniversary exhibit, but this action only drew the ire of historians who accused curators of bowing to political pressure and "cleansing" history.

Using the atomic bomb against Japan unleashed a Pandora's box of consequences that haunt the world to this day. When the Soviet Union announced in 1949 that they, too, had the atomic bomb, it sparked a nuclear arms race that lasted over three decades. It consumed billions of dollars, instilled in Americans and Russians a constant fear of mutual nuclear annihilation, and in 1962 brought the Soviet Union and the United States to the brink of nuclear war during the Cuban Missile Crisis. At the peak of the nuclear arms race, the Soviet Union and the United States combined had enough weapons to destroy the Earth hundreds of times over.

When the Soviet Union collapsed and fragmented in the late 1980s, it appeared that the menacing cloud of global nuclear destruction that had hung over the world for so long had finally lifted. The reality is that nuclear war is more of a probability now than it ever was. India and Pakistan, who have been fighting for decades over a disputed region called Kashmir, both possess a nuclear arsenal and have threatened to use them against each other if violence between the countries escalates to full-scale war.

Nations formerly part of the Soviet Union still possess nuclear weapons from the cold war era. Some of those countries are so ravaged by corruption and poverty that there is the very reasonable fear that they could sell the weapons to terrorist organizations or nations hostile to the United States. North Korea, a nation ruled by a ruthless and unpredictably dangerous dictator, has claimed to have detonated a nuclear weapon. Iran, a nation that has a long history of hostility toward Israel, the United States, and other countries, is believed to be in the process of developing nuclear weapons. The five acknowledged nuclear powers—the United States, Russia, China, France, and the United Kingdom—together possess thirty-one thousand nuclear weapons. Israel, surrounded by hostile nations in the Middle East, also possesses a nuclear arsenal. The threat of nuclear war is still a very real, frightening possibility. The devastation caused by these nuclear weapons would not, however, be limited to one nation as it was with Japan. With the sophisticated developments over the years in the destructive power and delivery capabilities, these weapons would have a global impact if used.

From 1945 until 1998, more than two thousand nuclear tests were conducted worldwide. In 1996 the Comprehensive Test Ban Treaty, a multilateral agreement signed by the United States, Confederation of Independent States (Russia and the former Soviet republics), the United Kingdom, and ninety non-nuclear-weapon states, banned all nuclear tests, above and below Earth's surface. It established a worldwide monitoring system to check air, water, and soil for signs of a nuclear explosion. To date, only twenty-six of the forty-four nations possessing some degree of nuclear capability have ratified the treaty. Although the United States signed, the Senate failed to ratify the treaty. India, Pakistan, and North Korea have neither signed nor ratified the treaty.

The International Atomic Energy Agency (IAEA) was established on July 29, 1957, to promote the peaceful use of nuclear energy and to discourage military use. Headquartered in Austria, the IAEA has 138 member states. It encourages the safe development of nuclear technology and safeguards against its misuse. As more countries began programs to develop nuclear technology, and possibly nuclear weapons, in the 1990s, the IAEA started to inspect these programs and investigate any suspected violations of the Nuclear Non-Proliferation Treaty.

Yet the proliferation of nuclear weapons is not the only problem that needs to be addressed. There is growing concern over the illicit trafficking of nuclear materials, especially since the fall of the USSR. According to the IAEA, nuclear materials such as natural uranium, depleted uranium, thorium, plutonium, and uranium enriched in the isotopes U-233 or U-235 are being sold or traded in the black market. The availability of plutonium and highly enriched uranium poses the greatest risk because they are used to produce nuclear weapons. As of December 31, 2001, IAEA listed 181 confirmed incidents involving the illicit trafficking in nuclear materials. Of these 181 incidents, seventeen involved either highly enriched uranium or plutonium.

The existence of nuclear weapons has led to other worries. Since 1950, there have been thirty-two known nuclear weapon accidents, which are known as "Broken Arrows." A Broken Arrow is an unexpected event involving nuclear weapons that results in the accidental launching, firing, detonating, theft, or loss of the weapon. By 2006, six nuclear weapons had been lost and never recovered.

But fully operable nuclear weapons are only part of the problem. There is also the danger of dirty bombs. A dirty bomb is a conventional

Published in November 1945, this cartoon entitled "Seeking Her Future" shows a young woman in Grecian garb, labeled "Civilization," gazing into a crystal ball labeled "Atomic Bomb." The drawing reflects the widespread concern people had for the future of civilization as they became aware of the destructive power of the atomic bomb. (National Archives)

explosive, such as dynamite, that is also filled with deadly radioactive particles. These particles scatter when the bomb goes off, spreading radiation over a large area. Such bombs could be miniature devices that would fit in a backpack or briefcase, or be as big as a truck. The likelihood of a nation unleashing nuclear weapons is greater now than it was during the cold war era.

"A Bomb" pin given to people who worked on the Manhattan Project (U.S. Department of Energy)

Postscript

On August 1, 1946, President Truman signed the Atomic Energy Act into law, placing America's nuclear research program under civilian administration. The governing body was called the U.S. Atomic Energy Commission, which later became the U.S. Department of Energy.

General Groves remained in charge of the Manhattan Engineer District until it was officially dissolved in 1947. He retired from the army with the rank of lieutenant general in 1948 and went to work in the private sector as a corporate executive. Harry S Truman was elected president of the United States in 1948 after finishing Roosevelt's term, but decided not to seek reelection in 1952. General Eisenhower succeeded him. Enrico Fermi, who led the group that created the world's first chain reaction on a squash court at the University of Chicago, went back to teaching after the war. Element 100 was named fermium (Fm) in his honor. Edward Teller, who advocated the building of more powerful bombs during the Manhattan Project, helped develop the hydrogen bomb and remained a vocal advocate throughout his career for more advanced thermonuclear devices. Leo Szilard, the leader of the so-called "Hungarian conspiracy" that lobbied President Roosevelt to start an atomic weapons program and who later led a campaign petitioning against using the bomb on Japan, left the field of physics for that of biology in 1947. With his friend Albert Einstein and other colleagues, Szilard continued to work toward peaceful uses of atomic energy and international arms control.

Albert Einstein always regretted the role he played in getting the Manhattan Project under way. In 1948 he declined an invitation to be the first president of the newly created state of Israel. Einstein spent his last years working with fellow scientists in a campaign to prevent the future use of nuclear weapons. Element 99 was named einsteinium (Es) in his honor.

Robert Oppenheimer, "Father of the Atomic Bomb," found himself the center of an international controversy in 1953 when he was accused of having Communist sympathies. Politicians like Senator Joseph P. McCarthy of Wisconsin, who exploited the fears of many Americans, helped fuel an anti-Communist paranoia that swept the nation, and reached a fever pitch in 1953. Oppenheimer's flirtations with the Communist Party in the 1930s came back to haunt him. The man who had led the most secret weapons development project in American history was stripped of his security clearance. Despite protests from the international scientific community, Oppenheimer's reputation suffered. In 1963 President Lyndon B. Johnson tried to redress this injustice by honoring Oppenheimer with the Atomic Energy Commission's prestigious Enrico Fermi Award.

The Department of Energy still maintains research facilities in the former Manhattan Project sites—the Oak Ridge National Laboratory, the Pacific Northwest National Laboratory in Hanford, and the Los Alamos National Laboratory. These facilities are centers for environmental, scientific, and technological research. Although Hanford is no longer engaged in nuclear weapons research, the Y-12 National Security Complex in Oak Ridge still produces components for thermonuclear weapons. Los Alamos National Laboratory continues to conduct research, development, and testing of nuclear weapons. There are several other facilities across the United States engaged in some phase of nuclear weapons research, development, and testing—the Pantex Plant in Texas, Lawrence Livermore National Laboratory and Sandia National Laboratories in California, and the Nevada Test Site sixty-five miles northwest of Las Vegas. To commemorate the sixtieth anniversary of the bombing of Hiroshima on August 6, 2005, simultaneous actions took place at these sites to protest the continuing involvement of the United States in nuclear weapons proliferation. Local antinuclear weapons organizations such as the Oak Ridge Environmental Peace Alliance (OREPA) organize activities throughout the year to educate people about nuclear weapons proliferation, including candlelight vigils held outside the gates of the Y-12 complex every Sunday at 5:00 P.M.

Hiroshima and Nagasaki are again thriving cities, but thousands of Japanese suffered for many years following the dropping of the atomic bombs. Those cities have the tragic distinction of being the only ones ever to be attacked by a nuclear weapon. For the sake of all humankind, we must hope this continues to be true.

Photography was severely restricted at Manhattan Project sites. Ed Westcott, pictured here in his darkroom, documented life and work at Oak Ridge. Many of his photographs are featured in this book. (U.S. Department of Energy)

Appendix: *Enola Gay* and *Bockscar* Flight Crews

Enola Gay Flight Crew

Navy Capt. William "Deak" Parsons, Manhattan Project Scientist
Sgt. Joseph S. Stiborik, radar operator
S./Sgt. George Robert "Bob" Caron, tail gunner
Pfc. Richard H. Nelson, radio operator
Sgt. Robert H. Shumard, assistant engineer
S./Sgt. Wyatt E. Duzenbury, flight engineer
Capt. Theodore J. Van Kirk, navigator
Maj. Thomas W. Ferebee, bombardier
Lt. Col. Paul W. Tibbets, 509th Group CO and pilot
Capt. Robert A. Lewis, copilot
Lt. Jacob Beser, radar countermeasures officer
Lt. Morris R. Jeppson, bomb electronics test officer

Bockscar Flight Crew

Maj. Charles W. Sweeney, aircraft commander

Capt. Charles D. Albury, copilot

Capt. James F. Van Pelt, navigator

Capt. Kermit K. Beahan, bombardier

2nd Lt. Fred J. Olivi, observer

M./Sgt. John D. Kuharek, flight engineer

Sgt. Raymond G. Gallagher, assistant engineer/scanner

Sgt. Abe M. Spitzer, radio operator

S./Sgt. Edward K. Buckley, radar operator

S./Sgt. Albert T. Dehart, tail gunner

Lt. Jacob Beser, radar countermeasures officer

Navy Cdr. Frederick C. Ashworth, weaponeer

Lt. Philip Barnes, assistant weaponeer

Chronology

1905

German physicist Albert Einstein publishes his theory of relativity regarding the convertibility of matter and energy ($E = mc^2$).

1933

January 30—Adolf Hitler is appointed chancellor of Germany.

1934

Italian physicist Enrico Fermi irradiates uranium with neutrons and unknowingly achieves the world's first nuclear fission.

1938

December—Otto Hahn and Fritz Strassmann successfully split uranium into two separate, lighter elements. The fission of uranium creates energy and additional neutrons, the basis of the atom bomb.

1939

September 1—Germany invades Poland. France and Great Britain, allies of Poland, declare war on Germany. World War II begins.

1940

Spring—Leo Szilard and Enrico Fermi receive a grant from the United States government to develop an atomic pile at Columbia University in New York City.

1941

December 7—Imperial Japanese naval forces launch a devastating surprise attack throughout the Pacific, including on Pearl Harbor naval base and other U.S. military installations in Hawaii.

December 8—The United States declares war on Japan.

December 11—Germany and Italy, allies of Japan, declare war on the United States.

1942

September 17—Leslie R. Groves is appointed director of the Manhattan Engineer District, later known as the Manhattan Project.

October—Groves appoints physicist J. Robert Oppenheimer scientific director of the Manhattan Project.

December 2—Under the direction of Enrico Fermi, the first sustained nuclear chain reaction is created on a squash court at the University of Chicago.

1943

April 15—Los Alamos, New Mexico, site begins operating.

Summer—Work begins on the implosion method for the plutonium bomb.

August—Plants at the Oak Ridge, Tennessee, site begin operations.

Fall—Construction of Hanford, Washington, facilities begins.

November 16—Heavy-water plant in Vemork, Norway, bombed in Allied air attack.

1944

February—Members of the Norwegian underground sink a ferry carrying heavy water to Germany.

November—Construction of Trinity test site begins in Alamogordo, New Mexico.

1945

April 12—President Roosevelt dies. Vice President Harry S Truman is sworn in as the thirty-third president of the United States.

May 7—Germany unconditionally surrenders to the Allies. The war in Europe ends.

July 16—A plutonium bomb nicknamed "the Gadget" is successfully tested at the Trinity site in Alamogordo, New Mexico.

July 26—President Truman issues the Potsdam Declaration calling for the unconditional surrender of Japan and warning of "utter destruction" if it does not comply.

July 26—The USS *Indianapolis* delivers the uranium-235 core manufactured at Oak Ridge for the "Little Boy" bomb. Four days later, the *Indianapolis* is sunk by a Japanese submarine.

August 6—*Enola Gay* drops the uranium bomb called "Little Boy" on Hiroshima.

August 9—*Bockscar* drops the plutonium bomb called "Fat Man" on Nagasaki.

August 15—Emperor Hirohito announces to the Japanese people the unconditional surrender of Japan.

1947

August 15—The Manhattan Project is officially dissolved with the establishment of the U.S. Atomic Energy Commission.

1949

August—The Soviet Union successfully tests an atomic bomb. The nuclear arms race begins.

1953

June 19—Ethel and Julius Rosenberg, convicted of passing nuclear secrets to the Soviet Union, are executed at New York's Sing Sing prison.

A billboard reminding Manhattan Project workers that their sacrifices are small compared to those of the soldiers fighting overseas (U.S. Department of Energy)

Process columns and racks at the S-50 plant in Oak Ridge, Tennessee
(U.S. Department of Energy)

Notes

Introduction WEAPONS OF MASS DESTRUCTION

p. 1 "The bomb . . ." quoted in Thomas and Morgan-Witts, p. 239.

p. 4 "A column of smoke . . ." quoted in Weale, pp. 130 and 136.

"Mission successful," quoted in Weale, pp. 139–140.

Although it has been mistakenly identified as *Boxcar* or *Bock's Car* in many historical accounts, the correct name of the plane that dropped the Nagasaki bomb is *Bockscar.* It is painted as one word on the fuselage.

One THE RACE FOR THE BOMB

p. 7 Fascism is a system of authoritarian government that developed in Europe during the twentieth century. Italy became the first Fascist nation in 1922 when Benito Mussolini became dictator. Nazi Germany (1933–1945) under Adolf Hitler was another Fascist nation, as were Hungary and Spain. To maintain power, Fascist regimes rigidly controlled culture and information and ruthlessly suppressed dissent.

p. 12 TNT is trinitrotoluene, a solid substance usually pale yellow to dark brown that is used as a high explosive.

p. 13 The "Final Solution" refers to the Nazi plan to systematically exterminate Jews. At least six million Jewish men, women, and children were murdered by the Nazis. In addition, millions of Gypsies, homosexuals, Jehovah's Witnesses, mentally and physically disabled individuals, political prisoners, and other "enemies of the state" were killed in the event that has come to be known as the Holocaust. To learn about the Final Solution and the Holocaust, read *Smoke and Ashes: The Story of the Holocaust* by Barbara Rogasky (New York: Holiday House, 2001).

p. 14 "At that time . . ." quoted in Weart, Spencer R., and Gertrud Weiss Szilard, eds. *Leo Szilard: His Version of the Facts: Selected Recollections and Correspondence* (Cambridge: MIT Press, 1978), p. 53.

p. 16 "[Einstein] was willing . . ." quoted in Feld, Bernard T., and Gertrud Weiss Szilard, eds. *The Collected Works of Leo Szilard* (Cambridge: MIT Press, 1972), Vol. II, p. 83.

"This new phenomenon . . ." quoted in Einstein, "Letter to Franklin D. Roosevelt," 2 August, 1939.

Two DANGEROUS SCIENCE

p. 18 "nuclear . . . limitless . . . unquenchable . . ." quoted in Wells, H. G. *The World Set Free* (New York: E. P. Dutton, 1914), p. 152.

p. 23 "the pile has . . ." quoted in Rhodes, pp. 439–440.

"I shook hands . . ." Ibid., p. 442.

Three THE MANHATTAN PROJECT

p. 25 "probably the angriest . . ." quoted in Rhodes, p. 424.

pp. 25-26 "[T]he biggest sonavabitch . . ." Ibid., p. 426.

p. 29 "He's a genius. . . ." Ibid., p. 448.

p. 32 "Bear Creek Valley . . ." quoted in Overholt, pp. 11–12.

"John Hendrix, Prophet of Oak Ridge, Predicted Project and Railroad More Than 40 Years Ago." *Oak Ridge Journal* (November 2, 1944): 3–4.

"Prophet's Vision Remembered." *Knoxville News-Sentinel* (January 22, 1984): E1–E2. There is no written evidence that Hendrix, who died in 1915, made these predictions since he never bothered to write them down. He simply told everyone he knew about his vision, and the story survived to become the stuff of local legend.

p. 32 "All the folks . . ." quoted in Johnson and Jackson, p. 41.

p. 36 "In March 1943 . . ." quoted in Sanger with Mull, p. 8.

p. 38 Plutonium (Pu) is a synthetic, radioactive metallic element used in nuclear reactors and nuclear weapons. Its atomic number is 94. Isotopes of plutonium were first identified in 1940 by the Manhattan Project scientist Glenn T. Seaborg and his associates at the University of California, Berkeley. The most important isotope, Pu-239, is produced by bombarding U-238 with slow neutrons. Pu-239 readily undergoes fission, so it is used in nuclear reactors to produce energy and in nuclear weapons to give them their explosive power.

Four Secret Cities, Secret Lives

p. 45 "I didn't run into . . ." quoted in Sanger with Mull, p. 105.

p. 51 "atmosphere of rudeness . . ." quoted in Overholt, p. 87.

pp. 52-53 "In order not to . . ." quoted in Johnson and Jackson, p. 19.

p. 53 "A lot of them . . ." quoted in Sanger with Mull, p. 85.

"'Twas on a hot . . ." Ibid., p. 47.

"The next morning . . ." Ibid., p. 89.

p. 54 "He concocted a mixture . . ." quoted in Overholt, p. 89.

Five Saboteurs and Spies

pp. 57-58 "We wore our badges . . ." quoted in Overholt, pp. 68–69.

p. 58 "You are now . . ." quoted in Johnson and Jackson, p. 150.

p. 61 "Everybody was spied upon," quoted in Sanger with Mull, p. 110.

"We did spot checks . . ." Ibid., p. 112.

p. 62 "I got calls . . ." Ibid., p. 111.

p. 65 "We understood how . . ." quoted in Rhodes, p. 456.

p. 68 "Moe was absolutely ideal . . ." quoted in Kaufman, Fitzgerald, and Sewell, p. 16.

p. 70 *Alsos* is a Greek word that means "grove." The mission name was a play on General Groves's name.

Six TRINITY

p. 82 "Batter my heart . . ." quoted in Donne, John. *Selected Poems,* ed. by Shane Weller (Mineola, N.Y.: Dover, 1993), p. 64.

p. 89 "We ourselves are . . ." quoted in Szasz, pp. 85–86.

"We were lying there . . ." quoted in Rhodes, p. 672.

p. 90 "And the thunder . . . I am become death. . ." Ibid., p. 675.

"Suddenly there was . . ." Ibid., p. 672.

p. 93 "Now we're . . ." Ibid., p. 675.

pp. 93-94 "The effects could . . ." quoted in Jungk, p. 201.

p. 94 ". . . of the medieval . . ." quoted in Sanger with Mull, p. 174.

pp. 94-95 "The Atomic Age . . ." quoted in Szasz, pp. 88–89.

p. 95 "I am sure . . ." Ibid., p. 89.

"At first I was . . ." Ibid., p. 90.

"Hell's broken out . . ." Ibid., p. 84.

"Several inquiries have . . ." Ibid., pp. 85–86.

p. 96 "had a new weapon . . ." quoted in Rhodes, p. 690.

Seven JUDGMENT DAY

pp. 100-101 "We the undersigned . . ." quoted in "A Petition to the President of the United States," 17 July, 1945. U.S. National Archives, Record Group 77, Records of the Chief of Engineers, Manhattan Engineer District, Harrison-Bundy File, folder #76.

p. 102 "We should have . . ." quoted in Wyden, p. 172.

p. 103 "nuclear Pandora's box . . . ," Ibid., p. 174.

p. 104 "There are no alternatives . . ." quoted in Rhodes, p. 692.

p. 105 "was never an issue," quoted in Wyden, p. 227.

p. 108 German cities were also subjected to ferocious bombing raids. On the night of February 13, 1945, hundreds of Allied bombers participated in an air raid on Dresden, Germany, a city of no military importance. The thousands of bombs dropped on that city ignited a firestorm, which demolished 80 percent of its buildings and killed 135,000 people. It took hundreds of planes and thousands of conventional bombs to destroy Dresden; however, Hiroshima, a city of comparable population and size, was devastated with a single bomb. That is an example of the power of a nuclear weapon.

Eight Rain of Ruin

p. 112 "The bomb you . . ." quoted in Weale, p. 130.

p. 113 "We are carrying . . ." Ibid., p. 135.

"It's Hiroshima," Ibid., p. 136.

p. 114 "Target visually bombed . . ." quoted in Wyden, p. 247.

"My God . . ." Ibid., p. 140.

"This is the greatest . . ." Ibid., p. 289.

p. 116 "Hiroshima suffered . . ." quoted in Hersey, p. 49.

"There was but . . ." quoted in official report of Lieutenant General Seizo Arisue.

pp. 117-118 "All buildings such . . ." quoted in Shohno, pp. 31–32.

pp. 119-120 Leaflets quoted in Manhattan Project Heritage Preservation Association, Inc. (MPHPA). www.childrenofthemanhattanproject.org/CG/CG_09B.htm.

p. 121 "All the buildings . . ." quoted in Sanger with Mull, p. 178.

p. 125 "I cannot bear . . ." quoted in Wyden, p. 302.

p. 126 "The time has . . ." Ibid.

"We are determined . . ." Ibid., p. 304.

p. 127 "I wish to . . ." Ibid.

"The enemy has . . ." Ibid., p. 305.

Nine AFTERMATH

p. 129 "The world is not . . ." quoted in "Death of a Genius," *Time* (2 May 1955): 4.

"Nobody is more . . ." quoted in Wyden, p. 294.

pp. 130-131 "too much gratification . . ." Ibid., p. 287. In 1942, following the surrender of the Philippines, the Japanese forced American and Filipino prisoners-of-war to march from the Bataan Peninsula to prison camps in the north. As many as ten thousand soldiers died of disease, starvation, beatings, and outright execution on what became known as the Bataan Death March.

"In August 1945 . . ." quoted in Thomas and Morgan-Witts, "Why We Did It," *Newsweek* (24 July, 1995): 22–23.

p. 132 "We worked . . ." quoted in Sanger with Mull, pp. 68–69.

"Excitement. We couldn't . . ." quoted in Overholt, p. 229.

pp. 132-133 "In front of . . ." Ibid., p. 231.

p. 134 "I voiced to . . ." quoted in Norris, p. 531.

"The use of . . ." quoted in Weale, p. 194.

p. 135 "The Manhattan Project . . ." quoted in Sanger with Mull, p. 177.

"I have no remorse . . ." quoted in Lamont, pp. 302–303.

"I have been asked . . ." quoted in Sanger with Mull, p. 177.

p. 136 "It was a question . . ." quoted in Lamont, p. 303.

p. 137 "There was never . . ." Ibid., p. 304.

"Certainly prior to . . ." quoted in Walker, Samuel J. "The Decision to Use the Bomb: A Historiographical Update." *Diplomatic History* 14 (Winter 1990): 110.

pp. 138-139 "From my point . . ." Excerpted from Press Release by Brigadier General Paul W. Tibbets (USAF Retired) for Airmen Memorial Museum, 9 June, 1994.

p. 139 The Cuban Missile Crisis began when the United States discovered that Cuba had secretly installed Soviet missiles capable of carrying nuclear weapons that would be able to reach most of the United States. The discovery led to a tense standoff over several days in October 1962 as the United States imposed a naval blockade of Cuba and demanded that the Soviets remove the missiles. This incident is regarded by many historians as the world's closest approach to nuclear war.

Postscript

p. 145 To learn more about the hydrogen bomb, read *Dark of the Sun: The Making of the Hydrogen Bomb* by Richard Rhodes (New York: Simon & Schuster, 1996).

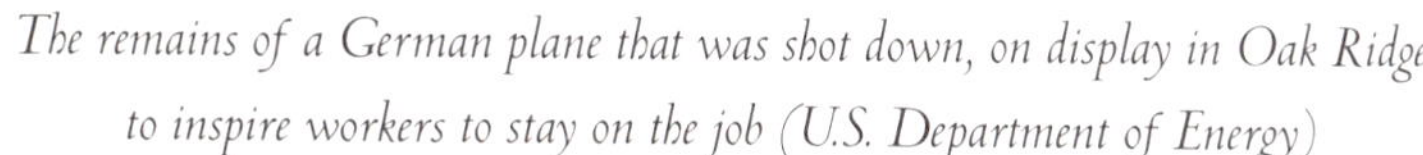

The remains of a German plane that was shot down, on display in Oak Ridge to inspire workers to stay on the job (U.S. Department of Energy)

Military police patrolling the Oak Ridge reservation in an armored car (U.S. Department of Energy)

Bibliography

Books

Akizuki, Tatsuichiro. *Nagasaki 1945.* London: Quartet Books, 1982.

Allen, Thomas B., and Norman Polmar. *Code-Name Downfall: The Secret Plan to Invade Japan and Why Truman Dropped the Bomb.* New York: Simon & Schuster, 1995.

Bernstein, Jeremy. *Oppenheimer: Portrait of an Enigma.* Chicago: Ivan R. Dee, 2004.

Bird, Kai, and Martin J. Sherwin. *American Prometheus: The Triumph and Tragedy of J. Robert Oppenheimer.* New York: Knopf, 2005.

Blow, Michael. *The History of the Atomic Bomb.* New York: Harper, 1968.

Dawidoff, Nicholas. *The Catcher Was a Spy: The Mysterious Life of Moe Berg.* New York: Vintage, 1995.

Fisher, Phyllis K. *Los Alamos Experience.* New York: Japan Publications, 1985.

Gallagher, Thomas M. *Assault on Norway: Sabotaging the Nazi Nuclear Program.* New York: Lyons Press, 2002.

Goodchild, Peter. *J. Robert Oppenheimer: Shatterer of Worlds.* Boston: Houghton Mifflin, 1981.

Groueff, Stéphane. *Manhattan Project: The Untold Story of the Making of the Atomic Bomb.* Boston: Little, Brown, 1967.

Groves, Leslie R. *Now It Can Be Told: The Story of the Manhattan Project.* New York: Harper, 1962.

Hachiya, Michihiko. *Hiroshima Diary: The Journal of a Japanese Physician, August 6–September 20, 1945.* Trans. Warner Wells, M.D. Chapel Hill: University of North Carolina Press, 1955.

Herken, Gregg. *Brotherhood of the Bomb: The Tangled Lives and Loyalties of Robert Oppenheimer, Ernest Lawrence, and Edward Teller.* New York: Henry Holt and Company, 2002.

Hersey, John. *Hiroshima.* New York: Vintage Books, 1946, 1985.

Johnson, Charles W., and Charles O. Jackson. *City Behind a Fence: Oak Ridge, Tennessee, 1942–1946.* Knoxville: University of Tennessee Press, 1981.

Johnson, Leland, and Daniel Schaffer. *Oak Ridge National Laboratory: The First Fifty Years.* Knoxville: University of Tennessee Press, 1994.

Jungk, Robert. *Brighter Than a Thousand Suns: A Personal History of the Atomic Scientists.* New York: Harcourt Brace, 1958.

Kaufman, Louis, Barbara Fitzgerald, and Tom Sewell. *Moe Berg: Athlete, Scholar, Spy.* Boston: Little, Brown, 1974.

Kurzman, Dan. *Blood and Water: Sabotaging Hitler's Bomb.* New York: Henry Holt and Company, 1997.

———. *Day of the Bomb: Countdown to Hiroshima.* New York: McGraw-Hill, 1986.

Lamont, Lansing. *Day of Trinity.* New York: Atheneum, 1965.

Lyon, Fern, and Jacob Evans eds. *Los Alamos: The First Forty Years.* Los Alamos, N. Mex.: Los Alamos Historical Society, 1984.

Mason, Katrina R. *Children of Los Alamos: An Oral History of the Town Where the Atomic Age Began.* New York: Twayne Publishers, 1995.

Morland, Howard. *The Secret That Exploded.* New York: Random House, 1981.

Nichols, K. D. *The Road to Trinity.* New York: William Morrow, 1987.

Norris, Robert S. *Racing for the Bomb: General Leslie R. Groves, The Manhattan Project's Indispensable Man.* South Royalton, Vt.: Steerforth Press, 2002.

Overholt, James, ed. *These Are Our Voices: The Story of Oak Ridge, 1942–1970.* Oak Ridge, Tenn.: Children's Museum of Oak Ridge, 1987.

Polmar, Norman. *The Enola Gay: The B-29 That Dropped the Atomic Bomb on Hiroshima.* Washington, D.C.: Brassey's, 2004.

Powers, Thomas. *Heisenberg's War: The Secret History of the German Bomb.* New York: Knopf, 1993.

Purcell, John Francis. *The Best-Kept Secret: The Story of the Atomic Bomb.* New York: Vanguard Press, 1963.

Rhodes, Richard. *The Making of the Atomic Bomb.* New York: Simon & Schuster, 1986.

Robinson, George O. *The Oak Ridge Story.* Kingsport, Tenn.: Southern Publishing, 1950.

Sanger, S. L., with Robert W. Mull. *Hanford and the Bomb: An Oral History of World War II.* Seattle, Wash.: Living History Press, 1990.

Selden, Kyoko, and Mark Selden, eds. *The Atomic Bomb: Voices from Hiroshima and Nagasaki.* Armonk, N.Y.: M. E. Sharpe, 1990, 1997.

Shohno, Naomi. *The Legacy of Hiroshima: Its Past, Our Future.* Tokyo: Kosei, 1986.

Smyser, Dick. *Oak Ridge 1942–1992: A Commemorative Portrait.* Oak Ridge, Tenn.: Oak Ridge Community Foundation, 1992.

Szasz, Ferenc Morton. *The Day the Sun Rose Twice: The Story of the Trinity Site Nuclear Explosion, July 16, 1945.* Albuquerque: University of New Mexico Press, 1984.

Szilard, Leo. *Leo Szilard: His Version of the Facts: Selected Recollections and Correspondence.* Eds. Spencer R. Weart and Gertrud Weiss Szilard. Cambridge, Mass.: MIT Press, 1980.

Takaki, Ronald. *Hiroshima: Why America Dropped the Atomic Bomb.* Boston: Little, Brown, 1995.

Thomas, Gordon, and Max Morgan-Witts. *Enola Gay.* New York: Stein and Day, 1997.

Tibbets, Paul W. *Return of the Enola Gay.* Columbus, Ohio: Mid-Coast Marketing, 1998.

Weale, Adrian, ed. *Eye-Witness Hiroshima: First-Hand Accounts of the Atomic Terror That Changed the World.* New York: Carroll & Graf, 1995.

Wyden, Peter. *Day One: Before Hiroshima and After.* New York: Simon & Schuster, 1984.

Suggestions for Further Reading

Coerr, Eleanor. *Sadako.* Illus. Ed Young. New York: G. P. Putnam's Sons, 1993.

———. *Sadako and the Thousand Paper Cranes.* Illus. Ronald Himler. New York: G. P. Putnam's Sons, 1977.

Cohen, Daniel. *The Manhattan Project.* Brookfield, CT: Millbrook, 1999.

Dower, John W. *Embracing Defeat: Japan in the Wake of World War II.* New York: W. W. Norton & Company, 1999.

Green, Connie Jordan. *The War at Home: A Novel.* New York: Margaret K. McElderry Books, 1989.

Grey, Vivian. *Moe Berg: The Spy Behind Home Plate.* Philadelphia: Jewish Publication Society, 1996.

Groueff, Stéphane. *Manhattan Project: The Untold Story of the Making of the Atomic Bomb.* Boston: Little, Brown, 1967.

Hersey, John. *Hiroshima* (New Edition). New York: Vintage Books, 1989.

Johnson, Charles W., and Charles O. Jackson. *City Behind a Fence: Oak Ridge, Tennessee, 1942–1946.* Knoxville: University of Tennessee Press, 1981.

Lace, William W. *The Atom Bomb.* San Diego: Lucent Books, 2001.

Lawton, Clive A. *Hiroshima: The Story of the First Atom Bomb.* Cambridge, MA: Candlewick Press, 2004.

Maruki, Toshi. *Hiroshima No Pika.* New York: Harper, 1982.

Overholt, James, ed. *These Are Our Voices: The Story of Oak Ridge, 1942–1970.* Oak Ridge, Tenn.: Children's Museum of Oak Ridge, 1987.

Powers, Thomas. *Heisenberg's War: The Secret History of the German Bomb.* New York: Knopf, 1993.

Rhodes, Richard. *The Making of the Atomic Bomb.* New York: Simon & Schuster, 1986.

Robinson, George O. *The Oak Ridge Story.* Kingsport, Tenn.: Southern Publishing, 1950.

Roleff, Tamara L. *The Atom Bomb* (Turning Point in World History). San Diego: Greenhaven Press, 2000.

Taylor, Theodore. *The Bomb.* San Diego: Harcourt Brace and Company, 1995.

Weale, Adrian, ed. *Eye-Witness Hiroshima: First-Hand Accounts of the Atomic Terror That Changed the World.* New York: Carroll & Graf, 1995.

Wyden, Peter. *Day One: Before Hiroshima and After.* New York: Simon & Schuster, 1984.

Yep, Laurence. *Hiroshima: A Novella.* New York: Scholastic, 1995.

Zindel, Paul. *The Gadget.* New York: HarperCollins Children's Books, 2000.

Websites

A-Bomb WWW Museum
www.csi.ad.jp/ABOMB

Albert Einstein Online
www.westegg.com/einstein

Alliance for Nuclear Accountability
www.ananuclear.org

Alsos Digital Library for Nuclear Issues
alsos.wlu.edu

Brigadier General Paul W. Tibbets (USAF Retired)
www.theenolagay.com

Bulletin of the Atomic Scientists
www.thebulletin.org

Leo Szilard Online
www.dannen.com/szilard.html

Manhattan Project Heritage Preservation Association
www.childrenofthemanhattanproject.org

Nuclear Bombs—How They Work
www.worsleyschool.net/science/files/nuclear/bomb.html

Nuclear Control Institute
www.nci.org

Nuclear Files
www.nuclearfiles.org

Trinity Atomic
www.cddc.vt.edu/host/atomic/trinity/tr_test.html

U.S. Department of Energy Office of History and Heritage Resources
www.cfo.doe.gov/me70/history/museums_and_pa.htm

A "Stay on the Job" rally in Oak Ridge (U.S. Department of Energy)

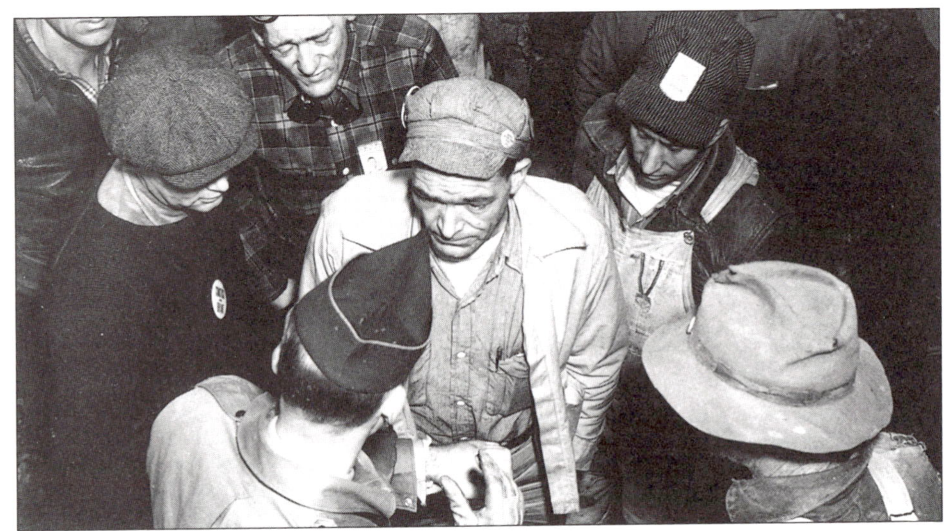

Glossary

atom—the smallest part of an element, made up of electrons, protons, and neutrons in various proportions, which are held together by a powerful force.

atomic bomb (A-bomb)—an extremely powerful explosive device that depends upon the release of energy from the splitting of atomic nuclei, or fission.

cadmium—a soft, bluish white metallic element. It is used in nuclear reactor shields.

centrifuge—a rotating vessel used when enriching uranium.

chain reaction—a self-sustaining process by which fission causes the release of neutrons in an atom, which in turn causes further fission. This chain reaction is the basis of both nuclear power and nuclear bombs.

control rods—devices that can be raised and lowered in the reactor core to absorb neutrons and regulate the fission chain reaction.

criticality—pertaining to a critical mass, the least amount of fissionable material that can achieve self-sustaining nuclear chain reactions.

critical mass—the minimum mass of a fissionable material that will maintain a fission chain reaction under precisely specified conditions.

deuterium—an isotope of hydrogen with one proton and one neutron in the nucleus, making this isotope about twice as heavy as normal hydrogen.

diffusion—a technique for uranium enrichment in which the lighter U-235 isotopes move through a porous barrier more rapidly than the heavier U-238 isotopes.

dirty bomb—a conventional explosive, such as dynamite, filled with radioactive particles, which scatter when the bomb denotates.

electromagnetic separation—the separation of uranium isotopes by electromagnetic means to produce U-235 for an atomic bomb.

electron—a particle of very small mass, carrying a negative charge. Electrons, which surround the nucleus, are present in all atoms; their number is equal to the number of positive charges (or protons) in the particular nucleus.

element—one of the distinct, fundamental varieties of matter, which, individually or in combination, compose all substances. Approximately ninety different elements are known to exist in nature. Several others, including plutonium, have been created as a result of nuclear reactions.

enrichment—the process of increasing the concentration of one isotope of a given element.

fission—the process whereby the nucleus of a particular heavy element generally splits into two nuclei of lighter elements, releasing substantial amounts of energy.

fission bomb—a nuclear bomb made by releasing energy through the fission (splitting) of heavy elements such as uranium 235 or plutonium 239.

flash burn—a burn caused by excessive exposure of skin to thermal radiation.

fusion—the process by which atoms are united in various combinations, which releases powerful energy. The hydrogen bomb (H-bomb) used fusion as the source of its explosive power.

fusion bomb—a nuclear bomb based on the fusing, or uniting, of light elements. Fusion bombs use fission bombs for ignition.

"the Gadget"—the atomic bomb tested at 5:29:45 A.M. on July 16, 1945, in Alamogordo, New Mexico.

ground zero (GZ)—the point on the surface of land vertically below or above the center of the explosion of a nuclear weapon.

gun-type weapon—a device in which two or more pieces of fissionable material, each less than a critical mass, are brought together very rapidly so as to form a supercritical mass that can explode as the result of a rapidly expanding fission chain reaction.

heavy water—water in which the hydrogen is composed of more than 99 percent deuterium atoms. The neutron in the deuterium nucleus allows this type of water to slow, or moderate, neutrons from fissioning uranium, permitting a sustained chain-reaction in reactors using natural uranium as fuel.

highly enriched uranium (HEU)—uranium in which the naturally occurring U-235 isotope—0.7 percent in natural uranium, 99.3 percent in U-238—is increased to 20 percent or above, but usually to 90 percent or more.

hydrogen bomb (H-bomb)—a nuclear weapon in which light atomic nuclei of hydrogen are joined together to release tremendous amounts of energy. The hydrogen bomb is approximately one thousand times more powerful than the atomic bomb.

implosion weapon—a device in which a quantity of fissionable material, less than a critical mass, has its volume suddenly decreased by compression so that it becomes supercritical and an explosion can take place.

isotopes—atoms that have the same number of protons but a different number of neutrons; that is, they are atoms of the same element that have different masses. Their atomic number (proton number) is the same, but their mass numbers (the total number of protons and neutrons in the nucleus) vary.

kiloton—approximately the amount of energy that would be released by the explosion of 1,000 tons of TNT.

moderator—a component of nuclear reactors that slows neutrons, increasing their chances of being absorbed by a fissile material. Natural water, heavy water, and nuclear-grade graphite are the most common moderators.

neutron—a neutral particle present in all atomic nuclei, except those of ordinary hydrogen. Neutrons are required to initiate the fission process, and large numbers of neutrons are produced by both fission and fusion reactions.

particle—a basic unit of matter.

pile—an older term for nuclear reactor.

plutonium (Pu)—a manufactured element produced when uranium is irradiated in a reactor. Plutonium 239 (Pu-239) is the most suitable isotope for constructing nuclear weapons.

proliferation—the spread of nuclear weapons to new countries.

proton—a particle of very small mass, carrying a positive charge.

radiation—the radiant energy emitted by certain elements such as radium, uranium, plutonium, and their products.

radioactivity—the spontaneous emission of radiation from the nucleus of an unstable isotope.

reactor—a facility that contains a controlled nuclear chain reaction. It can be used to generate electricity, conduct research, produce isotopes, and manufacture elements such as plutonium.

subcritical—an insufficient amount of mass to maintain a fission chain reaction.

supercritical—a quantity of fissionable material that is greater than the critical mass.

thermonuclear—using very high temperatures to bring about the fusion of light nuclei (hydrogen), which releases tremendous amounts of energy.

uranium 235 (U-235)—an isotope of uranium that is fissionable and can sustain a chain reaction.

uranium 238 (U-238)—the most common isotope of uranium. It is non-fissionable, but when irradiated by neutrons, it produces fissionable plutonium 239 (Pu-239).

uranium enrichment—the process of increasing the percentage of U-235 isotopes so that the uranium can be used as reactor fuel or in nuclear weapons.

Index

Page numbers in *italics* refer to illustrations.

I

J

K

L

M

N

O

P

R

Z

Aerial view of the K-25 plant in Oak Ridge, Tennessee.
At the time of its completion, K-25 covered more area than any other building ever built.
(U.S. Department of Energy)